ADVANCE PRAISE FOR
THE SAN FRANCISCO FALLACY

"A memoir of failure and success by a leading entrepreneur."
— **Neil Patel,** Co-Founder of Crazy Egg and Hello Bar

"A timely deconstruction of the San Francisco myth and other groupthink that afflicts tech startup culture. Jonathan gets real about what it takes to build a profitable business."
— **Murtaza Hussain,** Co-Founder of TwitchAlerts

"In his wonderful new book, Jonathan Siegel articulates persistent fallacies that bedevil modern entrepreneurs. Jonathan has made all the entrepreneurial mistakes and then some. Save yourself time, humiliation, and money and read The San Francisco Fallacy today."
— **Patrick Vlaskovits,** NYT Bestselling Author of Hustle and The Lean Entrepreneur

"San Francisco is Florence during the renaissance. But now the digital renaissance is spreading to all corners of the world. And that's where the opportunities are. Learn the fallacies of San Francisco so that you can avoid them, and get busy because the universe needs you to build what you have in your dreams, wherever you are."
— **Xavier Damman,** Co-Founder of Storify

"If you want to learn from one of tech's clearest minds, crack this book open and dive in. Jonathan's turned his laser focus on what matters into a repeatable recipe for big exits. Filled with refreshing thinking and a focus on what really drives profitable tech companies, this book grabs you by the collar, slaps you across the face, and yells in your face, "focus on what matters". Better yet, it tells you just how to do that. Every founder thinking of raising money needs to read this book before putting that first pitch deck together."
— **Doug Breaker,** CEO of Earth Class Mail

"A gripping perspective on the realities of success and failure following the life of one of the most extraordinary entrepreneurs out there. It is unique to find someone with this level of in-depth product knowledge and such strong commercial aptitude. With that blend it gives the reader quite a unique view into the thinking of such a talented individual with plenty of learnings to take away."
— **Paul Kenny** Award-Winning Serial Entrepreneur Based in the Middle East

D1082442

"I read every new, good book on startups that comes out. It's my job. And this is one of the best books I've read in a long time. The advice in The San Francisco Fallacies is priceless. Perhaps because it is so unobvious, yet so practical and proven. Jonathan is one of the most successful, unknown entrepreneurs in Silicon Valley. And he has done something different with this book. It's well written and entertaining. You can finish it in one sitting. And in that time your future will be changed. No entrepreneur can afford to miss this book because you won't find the same advice elsewhere. I'm not just saying this—the things I've learned from Jonathan have changed my life."

– Trevor Owens, Author of The Lean Enterprise

"Jonathan is a true entrepreneur with a passion for building and growing companies. With unique insights and experience in the Valley he has learned there are better ways and places to get things done—and that is what he does. In The San Francisco Fallacy, he spells out just what he has learned and how he applies it."

– David Hauser, Founder of Grasshopper

THE SAN FRANCISCO FALLACY

THE

SAN FRANCISCO

FALLACY

THE TEN FALLACIES THAT MAKE FOUNDERS FAIL

JONATHAN SIEGEL

WITH COLIN MURPHY

THE SAN FRANCISCO FALLACY
The Ten Fallacies That Make Founders Fail

ISBN   978-1-61961-632-5   *Paperback*
       978-1-61961-392-8   *Ebook*

INTERIOR DESIGN BY
Kevin Barrett Kane

LIONCREST
PUBLISHING

Starting a business is tough. Going through failure again and again can be soul destroying. Writing this book was, at times, my nemesis.

My adventures would not have been possible— and at best incomplete—without the unending support of my wife and family.

Thank you for suffering through my late nights and blurry eyes and giving me the push across the finish line. Again and again and again.

TABLE OF CONTENTS

THE SAN FRANCISCO FALLACY

I'VE LIVED AND WORKED in San Francisco. It's a beautiful city and a great place to party. But it's a lousy city to build a startup. Yet San Francisco is seen as the global epicenter of startup culture. Would-be founders flock there from all over the United States—and the world. Why?

Because they think, "If everybody else is doing it, then it must be the thing to do." *That's* the San Francisco Fallacy.

My businesses have been built out of Las Vegas, Santa Barbara, Ireland, and Poland. Each location, at the time, was cheaper than San Francisco *and* had more available talent.

When I built a team in Vegas, the city had 15 percent unemployment, a good supply of graduates, a great pipeline of experienced salespeople, a low cost of living, and tons of cheap property. (The entertainment's also pretty good.) Meanwhile, in San Francisco, rents were extortionate, talent was at a premium, and people were throwing fruit at the Google bus.

So why does everyone want to be in San Francisco? It's a nice place to live, no doubt, but nice rarely counts when it comes to the bottom line. Why would so many tech companies base themselves there?

This is the paradox of the tech identity: we consider ourselves outsiders; and we like to reinforce that by hanging out with our peers.

Startup founders like to think of themselves as pioneers out on the cultural frontier, even as they sit with their MacBooks and pour overs in a downtown coffee shop.

I get it. It feels good to be among our peers. It's reassuring. And it's exciting to be part of a "thing." It's only human. But it's bad business. Tech companies—particularly startups—are allowing their herd instincts to blunt their business sense.

The same groupthink and herd mentality that drives tech people to San Francisco in waves leads to other mistakes.

The "San Francisco Fallacy" is emblematic of a bubble mentality in the tech world. The truth is, even though as a group we like to think of ourselves as outliers, we are just as susceptible to conformist thinking as the mainstream.

I know I am.

Over my many years launching startups (sometimes succeeding, sometimes failing), I often fell victim to what I now recognize as a series of common errors—misconceptions that bedevil startup culture to this day. But I also learned how to sidestep and surmount many of these challenges.

This book is the distillation of that experience and learning.

Meeting young founders, giving talks, and my work as an angel investor made me think that the stories of my own successes and—crucially—failures would be worth writing down. As I wrote this story, I realized that those failures had common elements. And as I sought to model those common elements, the concept I fell upon was the "fallacy."

FALLACIES ARE COMMONLY HELD BELIEFS, or cultural norms, that turn out to be misguided or misleading. They may be explicit—things that people repeat to each other. ("Property prices only go up!") Or they may be implicit—codes of behavior that people don't articulate, and may even deny, but are visible to the outsider nonetheless.

Plenty of books will give you good advice on starting and

running businesses. Many of them will systematize this advice in a series of steps or stages or rules or a particular model. *The San Francisco Fallacy* is a little different. At its heart is a philosophy—of life as well as of business.

The book is not a step-by-step, how-to guide for a successful business. Nor is it an articulation of my foolproof strategies or carved-in-stone principles. Rather, it is a series of challenges to years of accumulated startup orthodoxy, written in the spirit of provocative "food for thought" for anyone who is trying to build a successful business.

In the following chapters, I attempt to debunk ten of the most deeply ingrained axioms within startup culture. I do so not to tear down but to build up, and to encourage a broader kind of critical thinking in all aspects of life.

We all subscribe to fallacies. I am coming to this book, and dissecting startups in this way, not because I have never made mistakes myself but precisely because I have—not just once but many times—and I have seen firsthand how conventional wisdom can be the path to failure.

IT ALL STARTS WITH MY FATHER. He was a specialist in nuclear safety—a very smart man. He got a PhD in nuclear physics and then an additional master's degree in nuclear engineering. He wanted to master the engineering part as well so that he could do the more practical aspects of nuclear physics—the implementation. He was inspired by a bigger goal, which was to make nuclear reactors safe.

We spent my early childhood, in the 1970s and 80s, living in Oak Ridge, Tennessee. My father had gotten a job there with a nuclear contractor, and my parents had bought a home. It was a good life. But then, on March 28, 1979, reactor number 2 of the Three Mile

Island nuclear power station in Pennsylvania failed, leading to a partial nuclear meltdown. The nuclear power industry found itself stalled; the Chernobyl disaster, just six years later, would send the industry into apparently irreversible retreat.

In the meantime, my father's contractor in Oak Ridge had lost its contract, and my father lost his job. Then the local savings and loan association collapsed. My parents lost their savings. In the resulting property crash, they lost all of the equity they had in their home.

We left Oak Ridge and crisscrossed the country, following my father in search of work. He picked up short contracts. In between, we went on food stamps. We had mason jars on the counter in the kitchen with labels taped to them saying, "Rent," "Groceries," "Movies," "Restaurant." When he got a paycheck, my father would cash it and divide the money between the jars. My siblings and I watched him, hoping the "Movies" jar would fill quicker.

In California, he found work as a substitute physics teacher in a private Catholic girls' school. The next term, the original teacher returned and, once again, he was unemployed. He got a job at the local Burger King. His former pupils found out. They used come by to see their former teacher flipping burgers. And to laugh.

Ultimately, he would find his new vocation as a teacher. But, in the meantime, they were tough years. As a child, it is hard to understand why your highly intelligent father can't get a job.

I was never ashamed of our relative poverty. I learned a lot about myself and my country by moving and having to change schools every year or two. In particular, there were very basic things I learned from my father's experience that are at the core of what I do now.

I learned the value of money: I learned to respect it, to spend it carefully, and to value it as a means to other ends. Being able to work and make money from that work became a very appealing scenario for me. Even as a child, I was drawn to activities and opportunities

that would generate revenue. And as I moved into the technology field, I was driven to create tech that was both useful and monetizable.

But I also learned from my father's experience that although there was virtue in working hard, being willing to do so was no guarantee of having work. And above all, I learned that you can't rely on the system. My father dedicated his life to critical thinking. He was a scientist, a trained skeptic. Yet he didn't apply that training to the norms of American society in the 1970s and '80s. Things that my father took to be true, and just, turned out to be fallacies. Believing them badly retarded his own career.

He had grown up during the baby boom years on the popular understanding that a good education would get you a good job, and a good job would be a job for life. If you studied and specialized and honed your skills and were willing to work hard, American society would have a place for you. The market would value your skill set and reward it. This was probably still true when he started college. It was no longer true by the time he was an early-stage career scientist with a young family to feed.

5

He didn't get the message that nuclear power was something the market didn't then want. He continued to look for opportunities in the space of nuclear safety, but the jobs had all dried up.

Perhaps there was nothing he could have done about it. Still, it seemed to me, as a boy, that he had been badly failed by the system to which he had devoted his adult life. He had been led to believe that all his studying and hard work in his early career would entitle him to a basic degree of security and fulfillment. Instead, he got food stamps.

IT'S NOT JUST PEOPLE WHO MAKE MISTAKES. Societies and cultures can make mistakes too. I first learned that observing my father.

These mistakes are usefully thought of in terms of "fallacies": fault lines in our culture; not merely one-off mistakes, but running sores. Two decades in tech startup culture has taught me that there are fallacies that are particular to this world—though, doubtless, many of them will recur in other business and management environments. This book is a bid to identify those key fallacies that dog startup culture.

The San Francisco Fallacy is the simplest and most obvious of these, which is why I took it as the rubric for this book. In my own experience and watching the experiences of others, I have found ten further fallacies that recur with frightening consistency and scupper otherwise-smart startups by people who should know better. These, then, are the ten fallacies that make founders fail.

FALLACY ONE: THE TECH FALLACY

THE TECH FALLACY

(AND HOW I FAILED AS A PORNOGRAPHER)

"It's all about the tech."

THE TECH FALLACY is perhaps the most pervasive fallacy in the tech world. It is endemic and insidious—perhaps inextricable. It first tripped me up as a teenager in my very first tech venture—but that wasn't enough to cure me, for I have fallen victim to it often since then.

The Tech Fallacy says it's all about the tech. Tech is the be-all and end-all of what we do. Get the tech right and the rest will follow.

This belief is deeply, badly wrong—as I first discovered in my teens.

HOW I FAILED AS A PORNOGRAPHER

My first tech business was a kind of online forum. It was called a bulletin board system, where members could chat and share software. It failed.

I launched my second online business two years later. It was another bulletin board system where members could chat and share software. Oh, and they could download porn.

I have my parents to thank for my incipient career as a pornographer. My father bought me my first computer in 1989, during one of his periods of regular employment.

It was an IBM clone with 640 kilobytes of ram and a 20-megabyte hard disk that weighed at least ten pounds. It had less power and memory than today's inkjet printer.

The PC had a menu of random shareware on it: one of the most popular was called Lena.exe. It was just a grainy, scanned image of a Playboy Bunny (albeit fully clothed). You ran the program, and it pushed the pixels slowly onto the screen. It took minutes to load the full picture.

I soon outgrew the menu on the machine, and then I went exploring. The operating system, MS-DOS 3.0, came with a manual. I read it. I learned every command. I saw that there were things called "batch files." I broke them open. This broke the computer. I watched it being fixed. I learned how to fix it myself (which was useful, because I kept breaking it). I learned how to write batch files.

I did regular teardowns of my machine. The pieces were on big chips with big pins and on full-size circuit boards over a foot in length. With two screwdrivers, I could unscrew, unstrap, and pry apart everything but the few capacitors and resistors soldered to the emerald-green, silicon circuit boards.

Computers were so young then that it wasn't clear to us what could go wrong, or why things broke. Disks would stop working and then work again. Displays wouldn't display in one mode, but work in another. Reset a switch or copy a file and all would be mysteriously better. When something went wrong, it took laborious practice, by trial and error, to find the source of the problem.

This early digital technology was, in fact, fantastically unpredictable. It seemed magical that it worked at all, and as I developed my understanding of how it did work, my respect for that underlying magic increased.

I got into code. Like Neo learning to watch the Matrix, at first I just saw scrolling screens of ostensibly incomprehensible characters; gradually, I began to see patterns and life in them.

I started to search out greater challenges and discovered the bulletin board system (BBS) – a rudimentary precursor to the Internet. A modem was used to dial into a BBS at the cost of a normal call. The BBS allowed you to create a user profile, message others, chat in forums, download free software (shareware), and play games such as Trade Wars—a cheesy, text-based, space-frigate game.

The bulletin boards were a fertile environment for viruses, which spread easily via shareware. As a result, one of the highly sought early pieces of shareware was McAfee's Virus Scanner, created by John McAfee in the 1980s.

McAfee uploaded his homemade virus scanner from his home to a local BBS, and it spread.

But McAfee's shareware was also a currency in itself. If you met someone on a BBS and she mentioned that she had McAfee 2.052, and you had McAfee 2.088, then you had currency to trade with.

The bulletin boards placed tight restrictions on how many files you could download: typically, you had to upload one file to be allowed to download three – ensuring sustainability and growth for the BBS. So if you had some shareware that a BBS didn't have, that would allow you to download three new pieces of shareware. And you could then use that to get new shareware from other bulletin boards.

But this was a different era of telecommunications, before cell phones. Landline calls within your local area were free, but long-distance calls were expensive. So if the BBS was locally-based, you could dial in for free; if it was further away, the cost would quickly get prohibitive – especially as downloads could take hours.

This created a market for more locally available software—a shareware broker. Local bulletin boards would set up to fill this market gap by downloading shareware from a distant BBS and providing it to local users for a subscription fee.

Most of these subscription bulletin boards provided a minimal free allowance to nonsubscribers, and because there was often more than one BBS within your toll-free zone, it was possible to seek out and trade shareware between boards. It was a classic network effect, with shareware spreading rapidly and efficiently at very low cost.

Then I saw an ad for a BBS in Sacramento that charged $60 per year and had twenty thousand subscribers. I thought I had misread it—$120,000 per year? For running a BBS—that is, for keeping a computer and a modem plugged in?

"I could do that!" I thought. And so I did.

Before long, I was hovering in front of my monitor late into the night, watching users work away on my BBS. In those days, you could see the screen your users saw and what they typed. "Analytics" meant staring at the monitor and watching what they were doing.

I added a notice to the BBS that came up upon login that said I would accept donations. In June 1991, I got my first check in the post for $20.

I thought it would be the first $20 of $120,000. But it turned out to be one of the only checks I received. And it took me another year, and the onset of puberty, to realize that the distant BBS in Sacramento had another section in its files area—one I hadn't previously discovered.

This wasn't freeware. It was photos. Lots and lots and lots of photos. Salacious, compromising, illicit photos. There were even a few with crude, jiggly animations of bits bobbing to and fro.

The clue was in the ad, but I had missed it. I had thought the "XXX" was just some elementary formatting.

I had been duped by my prepubescent naivety. It wasn't the pleasure of using my BBS that people were willing to pay for; it was an altogether more adult pleasure.

My excitement for the BBS drained. I shut it down and asked my mother to help me find a job. She took me to McDonald's.

I came home in despair, sat down at the kitchen table, and took up the phone book. This was in the Bay Area, so there were pages of computer companies. I started calling. But I was a kid and nobody took me seriously. I kept calling.

Finally, somebody listened, invited me in for a chat, and eventually offered me a job. The company was called ZOZ Computers. I had cold-called my way right through the phone book.

Months into this first employment, I told my new boss about my BBS failure. I wanted to beat my competitors at their own game.

"What's stopping you?" he asked.

"I'm too young to buy porn," I said.

"I'll buy it for you," he replied.

He ordered a set of CDs with porn images. I bought a six-disc CD changer for my computer and had three phone lines installed in my bedroom with modems. My mother was working long hours at the time and didn't notice.

I had built myself a 386 computer and put my old 286 to work answering the phones. One Saturday in 1993, I announced my new BBS via a $15 ad in the local computer trader paper.

Like sixteen-year-olds all over the United States that weekend, I spent a lot of time in my bedroom because of porn. But I suspect there were few others—if any—whose interest was more entrepreneurial than voyeuristic. Though I was a voyeur too, in a sense—stalking my users as they navigated my BBS.

From the moment the red LED lights on the modems first lit up and the modem started to whir, signaling an incoming call, I was hooked to my screen, fascinated by what those callers were doing. When the lights came on, I felt a surge of pride and accomplishment; when they hung, indicating that the system had crashed, I felt a profound sense of failure.

Users could get three photos a day for free, limited to ten a month, and they were limited to two hours in total online in a month. If they attempted to exceed that, they'd get a message: subscribe.

In order to become a subscriber, they had to download a pack of documents and sign and return them to me with a check: $35 per year. I remember watching my first pack being downloaded and the buzz of thinking, here comes my first customer.

I was aiming for one thousand subscribers. I had the latest tech, decent design, and a good stock of images. But six weeks later, I had made just over $400.

I had no ability to charge credit cards and was relying on people to send checks. Not having a credit card myself, because I was sixteen, it hadn't occurred to me that I'd need to process credit cards.

Still, I was giddy with success and wanted to share it. I confided in one of the adults I respected, my mother's landlord. He told her. She wasn't so thrilled that her teenage son was a pornographer (and she wasn't so impressed by the distinction between a pornographer and a pornography trader, either). She told me to shut it down. Between that and the too-slow income stream, I decided not to argue my First Amendment rights. At age sixteen, I'd notched up my second tech failure.

THE TECH FALLACY REVISITED

Selling porn taught me about the Tech Fallacy. I had believed that building great technology must mean that you're building a great business. That it was all about the tech.

But selling porn taught me that the raison d'être for any business is to give the customer what he wants. He doesn't want the tech; he wants what the tech can deliver. The tech is just the means to an end.

I thought I could make money from a well-built-and-run bulletin board system; however, decoding those ads in the computer trader papers with their XXXs made me realize that the market was more interested in the XXX than the BBS.

I love good tech. But I've learned to follow the good business. It's a better path.

Take two rival companies. Each is armed with $1 million in investments. One spends $900,000 on its technology development, with $100,000 reserved for going to market (i.e., customer development, sales, and marketing). The other spends $100,000 on technology and $900,000 on going to market.

Who wins? The market-driven one does. It's not the better product that wins; it's the product that best knows how to reach its market.

If a thriving company made you its CEO and you decided to let go of its sales and marketing divisions to focus more on the technology, the board would fire you. But walk into almost any two-year-old funded startup, and you'll see a growing development team budget and a speck, if any, allotted to sales and marketing.

Imagine an upstart competitor trying to challenge an entrenched leader without a sales and marketing division—it would be like a one-legged man in an ass-kicking contest.

Yet in the startups that I encounter, if the company has a team of ten, there'll be nine developers and just one person who is business driven. Contrast that with companies that have gone public: you'll see ninety salespeople for ten developers.

Why is this? Partly, it's intrinsic. People who love what they do often prefer to do it to the exclusion of other things and may not even realize they're doing this. Tech companies tend to be founded by people who love tech. A single-minded focus on the tech is to be expected but guarded against.

But it's also a feature of the zeitgeist—the spirit of the times. This takes us back to the first dot-com era. As we'll see later, the dot-com bubble was characterized by a focus on the *idea* to the exclusion of all else—even the tech (see Fallacy Six).

When that bubble burst, it left a bad taste in people's mouths, especially in the investment community. Tech startups acquired the reputation of being charlatans—all talk, no substance.

This perception created a pendulum swing: today, the emphasis in the startup market is often on developing innovative, hardcore technology, with a consequent failure to consider other crucial (maybe more crucial) aspects of the business.

There is a happy medium. Tech is helping to redefine how the world works—how we work and play, find our soul mates and flings, tell our stories, and hail a ride. Tech is required to catalyze these shifts and disruptions. We all love good tech.

But the winners will be those who build the best businesses, not the best tech.

TAKEAWAY: HOW TO AVOID THE TECH FALLACY

- Beware your infatuation with tech. Make sure you don't lose sight of your market.

FALLACY TWO: THE DEMOCRACY FALLACY

THE DEMOCRACY FALLACY

(AND HOW I LOST TO THE VIDEO GAME)

"Everything is awesome when you're part of a team."

I ONCE HEARD A THEORY that college makes us all, in effect, socialists. We learn to respect our peers; we learn to form groups; we learn how to cooperate. We form fast friendships. We leave college wanting to establish communities, not dictatorships. So when we set up companies, we do it as a team. Which can be awesome—until things go wrong.

The Democracy Fallacy is the belief that everything is awesome when you're part of a team; or, more prosaically, that team members should have an equal say—and stake—in your venture.

There are plenty of organizational and management theorists out there who will argue why equality boosts productivity, and they draw on the rare examples of cooperative businesses that hold their own in the marketplace as evidence. Perhaps that can work. And, no doubt, when it does work, it must be pretty awesome. But if it works, it works rarely.

More often, a flawed ethos of shared ownership and responsibility gets in the way of decision making and accountability. Businesses need leadership. Leaders need to be rewarded. All the more so in youthful startups.

I had a rude awakening in my first startup after college.

HOW I LOST TO THE VIDEO GAME

Sam, Chris and I started brainstorming technology ideas as soon as we graduated from college. Sam, an artist, was to be the CEO and creative lead while Chris and I were the developers. But, of course, the title "CEO" was only nominal: this was a team effort. We were equal partners (and equal equity holders) and intended to run the company more as a cooperative.

We were twenty-one-year-old tech nerds. Inevitably, our ideas revolved around one thing: video games. We were the first generation of kids with video games as a part of our childhood.

In 1998, the market for games was mainly on home consoles—Nintendo and Sega—and the PC market was just coming alive. That year, for the first time ever, the video game industry made the same amount of money as Hollywood.

The PC gaming market was accessible to young programmers, and it had a lower barrier to entry than consoles. *Civilization, Warcraft II,* and *Doom* were the dominant games, and there was a sense in the air that games were a coming force in both technology and culture. We wanted to push the boundaries of both technology and gaming. We decided to build a PC game that would be revolutionary: a 3-D military strategy game set in a medieval world that would allow many players to interact using a server—what would become known as a "massive multiplayer online role-playing game."

The life was intense, but simple. I went straight to the computer when I woke up, ate at it, and broke just for a brief game of pickup basketball on a court around the corner before working late into the night and then catching a few hours' sleep. We put in twenty-hour days and did that for eight months.

But the challenge was overwhelming: we realized we needed more time and that meant we needed money. We needed investors. We budgeted for four basic salaries for nine months, rent, computers, and the license for a design program: $90,000.

But because our game wasn't yet playable, we needed an alternative product to lure in potential investors. So we decided to build a quick, 2-D demo inspired by Sid Meier's *Alpha Centauri*.

Chris and I wrote code for thirty-six-hours straight. By then we had the bones of a new demo game. We called it *Conspire*. We were ready to pitch. But I had no idea who to pitch to, or how. So we started with people we knew: family, former teachers, ex-bosses. They pushed us on to people they knew. If anyone showed some interest, we offered to come to them. We drove to each potential investor, meeting them at their homes or at the local diner, across the length and breadth of California, from Los Angeles to Sacramento. We had a presentation, a budget, a business plan, and the demo.

We valued the company at double the investment we were seeking. Within days, we had raised the $90,000: twelve investors contributed between $3,000 and $30,000 each. After years of youthful obsession and now eight months of impoverished (but exciting) grind, I finally had some "real-world" endorsement. Serious people had invested their money in my partners and me. It was time to scale up.

We threw on utility belts to fit out our garage as an office. We posted ads for interns at the local community college and quickly found ourselves turning away would-be game artists and developers by the dozen. We grew our team to four employees and eight die-hard interns, and we sweated through long days at our desks, eating and sleeping in the garage. We returned to working on our 3-D medieval strategy game, but soon realized the challenge was far more complex than we had envisaged. Even with additional manpower, we were moving too slowly to produce anything within our nine-month window.

We went back to the 2-D demo, *Conspire*, and realized we could crank that out as an initial offering to the market. That made business sense: it would reduce the workload for the developers dramatically. But Sam, the artist at our helm, disagreed. He thought we were selling out, and that delivering a 2-D game to a market that was beginning to demand 3-D would be pointless.

He was nominally the CEO. But we were effectively a collective and considered it a point of pride that we did things by consensus or—on rare occasions—voted on them. We put it to a vote. Sam lost. We went ahead with the plan to release the 2-D game, and Sam rapidly became disillusioned.

For weeks, the team walked around on eggshells, surreptitiously trying to encourage Sam to either get enthused again or opt out altogether. Nobody was willing to confront him. We were a team, after all—we were in this together. We relied on solidarity, not authority, to get things done.

Eventually, I realized I was going to have to step up to the plate. I volunteered to talk to him. We sat down in my small study off the garage office. I was sweating and my heart was pounding.

In every scenario that I had played through in my head, Sam would inevitably be offended and get defensive. There would be conflict. I didn't like conflict. I wasn't confident that I'd handle it well. I tried to be straight up. "Sam, you were a superb designer and leader when we created the company a year ago," I said. "But over the past two months, that fire has gone out of you. I don't know if you recognize it, but it is gone." He did recognize it. In fact, he had been going through similar agony on his own, trying to work out how to resolve his discomfort with the company.

A year into a long-hours, low-pay startup project, he was disillusioned by the low return and frustrated that his peers elsewhere were getting paid far more for doing far less, in relatively secure employment. And he fundamentally disagreed with the direction we'd taken. So he welcomed the out, and he worked hard to facilitate our attempts to change and grow the company. His leaving cleared the air - but it left us with a hole where our creative engine had been.

We slogged on, developing the video game, but without Sam's innate sense of both aesthetics and drama, our progress was bloodless. We went back to basics. We reviewed every game we loved and tried to identify the key components that made them stand out. We went through the James Bond back catalogue, renting a movie a day, to mine them for plot ideas and to hone the sense of conspiracy. Those films made it clear where we were going wrong.

The best Bond films were the early ones, with Sean Connery smiling wryly as he left a trail of implicit destruction in his wake, rather than Roger Moore struggling with a laser gun in a spaceport. We had been building the video game equivalent of *Moonraker*, when what we wanted was *Dr. No*.

But we couldn't fix it. We tried everything we could think of to hone that sense of playability: we played every board game and card game we could find, as well as video games, but it evaded us. We didn't have the creative spark. It had been extinguished when Sam left.

We got stuck in a downward spiral, working harder and longer hours, under more pressure, dulling our creativity even further, all the while failing to face up to the reality.

I had risen to de facto CEO in the business. I was responsible for investor expectations and desperately wanted to meet them. But our costs were exceeding our budget. I was faced with shuttering the business or seeking more capital. That, though, is the story of the next chapter.

THE DEMOCRACY FALLACY REVISITED

Larry Ellison, Michael Dell, Bill Gates, Steve Jobs, Mark Zuckerberg…
None of them ever found themselves agonizing over team conflict.

Perhaps that was because they were all college dropouts. They weren't trying to build great peer environments where everyone could thrive together.

These founders didn't get fully baked into the "equal equity" tendencies that I found myself (and other founders) mired in. Or maybe they just had an astute and aggressive internal compass for leadership.

Sharing power and trying to make everyone happy diminishes the ability to take bold risks and make bold decisions.

People think visionary leadership is about convincing the markets. But you need strong leaders to take the kinds of stances and make the kinds of choices that are often unpopular *within* their companies.

Take the iPod Shuffle—a product that makes no sense. Apple launched the Shuffle at a time when everyone else was adding more displays, more information, more features to their MP3 players. In contrast, Apple took away every single feature that you'd expect. All that remained was one button, PLAY/PAUSE, and with that button you got random music. You could not choose what you were going to listen to. They took a ridiculous lack of features, an almost insulting lack of features, and sold that as a benefit – with extraordinary success.

This was only possible because of the single-minded focus of Jobs's leadership: no committee would ever have let the Shuffle come to market in such a competitive environment. Under a company that subscribed to the Democracy Fallacy, this simply wouldn't have been allowed.

It was essential that one leader be given the power and authority to make such a big, unlikely move.

And with such power should come disproportionate equity. Having a leader with a disproportionate shareholding means that there is someone anointed with the power and authority to make bold decisions.

If that person is wrong, it is clear that he or she is responsible and can quickly be brought to task. If the leader is right, then he or she can continue to rally internal and external support and execute efficiently. Sharing roles and equalizing power diminishes the ability to take risks. And it dilutes the trail of responsibility if things aren't working.

If you find yourself down the path to forming a company with equal shareholders, here's a good question to ask of each of the team: can they leave, and the business survive? Whose departure would cause the company to collapse?

At an early stage, everyone feels vital—your programmer is needed to write the code, your artist to do the design, your hustler to win your first sale. But, depending on your business, you may be able to pay a little more and get a contractor if your developer leaves. It hurts, but it doesn't kill the business.

There is always one person who holds the key to investment, who rallies the team – the person who acquired the first hundred customers. If that person leaves, the company dies, and you can't just replace him or her. *That* person needs to be your majority shareholder.

In my games studio, with the equity evenly shared among the three founders, we had stripped our CEO of the ability to flex his muscle. We had the ability to vote him out and, once we did, we failed.

THE LESSON FOR YOUNG, WOULD-BE FOUNDERS IS THIS: by all means, start a business with your friends. Fellowship may be the crucial ingredient that gets you through the ardors and ordeals of making a startup work. But you and your friends need to know where the buck stops. There needs to be a *primus inter pares*—a first among equals.

And that role is not merely a title or a casting vote if there's a tie. That role is the boss.

And that should be reflected in the equity. Otherwise, the equity will be a brake on the business and could ultimately break it.

I routinely speak with worried founders, anxious about a departing teammate and the impact that will have on the company's capitalization table. Not only can working that out be complex and stressful, but the prospect of having a cofounder with a large equity stake outside of the business—and possibly estranged from it—can act as a deadweight on the business, both for management and for potential investors. Avoid this from the beginning by creating a clear hierarchy of leadership and equity.

TAKEAWAY: HOW TO AVOID THE DEMOCRACY FALLACY

- Don't be seduced by the fraternity of teamwork. This is a business, not a sport. Businesses need leaders. And leaders need to be rewarded.

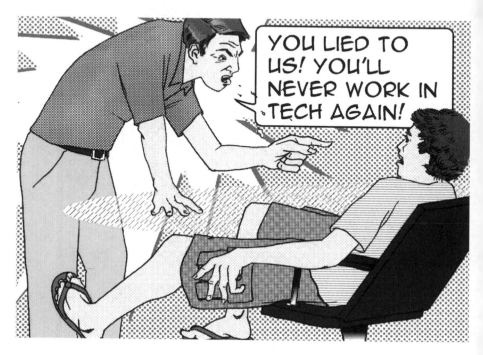

FALLACY THREE: THE INVESTMENT FALLACY

THE INVESTMENT FALLACY

(AND HOW I FAILED AS A DOT-COM KID)

"Raising money from investors is a mark of success."

SUCCESS STORIES *like these are a staple of the tech press:*

DOCUSIGN DOUBLES VALUATION TO $3 BILLION WITH $233 MILLION RAISE

INSTACART VALUED AT $2 BILLION IN NEW $220 MILLION FUNDRAISING

TWILIO HAS JOINED THE UNICORN RANKS WITH STEALTHY $100 MILLION RAISE

The numbers are big, the companies sound sexy, the tone of the stories is normally adulatory... This is success, right?

Wrong. The idea that raising investment is a mark of success—and a badge of honor—is the Investment Fallacy. Investment is a burden as much as—or more than—an opportunity. It increases the pressure, corrupts your incentives, and creates a communications minefield. Court it at your peril.

I learned that soon after I took over as de facto CEO of our games studio.

HOW I FAILED AS A DOT-COM KID

"You've been misappropriating funds," said the VC. "And you lied to us."

"You tell people what they want to hear even when you have to lie to do it," said his co-investor. He stuck the knife in deeper. "You've got some deep psychological flaw in there that you need to deal with." Then the VC delivered the coup de grâce: "You'll never work in technology again. We'll make sure of that."

It was about a year after I graduated school, in 2000, and we were sitting in a glass-walled conference room in a complex on Berkeley's University Avenue.

The VCs were in their late forties or fifties; I was twenty-two. They were wearing smart, business-casual threads. I was wearing shorts and sandals.

They were respected men of status in their communities; I was an upstart kid working from a garage. They were wealthy; I was broke. When they said I was finished, I believed them. I was scared. Scared but defiant. "If I've done anything wrong," I said, "I'm willing to go to jail." But inside I was beaten.

I had spent the best part of a year working crazy hours for a derisory paycheck on a project those men had agreed to fund. Suddenly, it had gone wrong. Trust had collapsed. How did it get to that?

WHEN SAM WALKED OUT OF OUR GAMES STUDIO, we lost our creative engine. He was designer, cofounder, and one-time CEO. His loss was a huge blow. We struggled to reenergize. We remained committed to our vision of producing a groundbreaking video game, but I could feel it receding fast.

And then we received an approach from a senior investor. Instead of investing in our games studio, he wanted us to merge into a new company, using his (better-paid and harder-hitting) lawyers. He was more interested in our skills as developers than our ideas for games.

We were fighting an uphill battle with the game, he argued, pursuing a product that may have been inspiring but promised little real chance of a return. Meanwhile, millions of dollars were being poured into ridiculous Internet startups.

Dump the game and start an Internet company, he said. In ten months, you'll be a millionaire. He flew in an ex-McKinsey consultant from New York to back him up. They won me over.

We brainstormed ideas and focused in on the area of sports statistics. One of our team members had made statistical reports for his local hockey league, and we decided to do the same thing online, but on a much wider scale. And so ScoreKeep.com was born.

Every hockey match, even in a local league, has a scorekeeper who records who scored each goal, who was in the rink when the goal was scored, who fouled, and other key stats. Our idea was that these stats could be easily entered online from report forms faxed in from the rinks, generating league reports automatically.

With player-level stats, this would produce custom dashboard reports of each individual player's performance, ranking, and development.

We successfully rolled out ScoreKeep.com for a local hockey league and then won a contract to service the California Community College basketball leagues. The NCAA invited us to consult on their operation. We were flown to Indianapolis, Indiana, to witness their set of eight industrial fax machines ringing nonstop as coaches at the top colleges sent in their stats.

This should have been exciting startup stuff, and yet I was becoming disillusioned. I was a good innovator, a good mobilizer, and a passionate programmer. I had proven to be good at getting in investments, not because of any experience with investors or talent for selling, but because I was super keen and knew my material. But those weren't the skills I needed to *manage* that investor engagement.

My new investors, the VC and his partner, had brought funding to the company and had agreed to look after the investors we'd recruited previously, to whom I felt a more personal commitment. (After all, I'd pitched the company to many of them in their homes, and they wrote personal checks.)

But that didn't happen. I gradually realized I had signed up for a project where the investors I had personally recruited were to be effectively abandoned in favor of a set of investors to whom I felt no connection or personal responsibility.

Eventually, trust broke down completely between the VC and me. I decided to leave, packed the company papers into a series of file boxes, and drove to their Berkeley offices to hand them over. I knew they wouldn't be happy—I just hadn't realized quite how aggressive they would be.

With the VC's threats that my career was over ringing in my ears, I left that office defeated and depressed.

Afraid of the prospect of a lawsuit, or worse, I called our district attorney and asked him if I had broken the law. He told me to stop wasting his time.

Slowly, I started to relax. A few months later, I wrote a cover story for a top tech journal. Nothing earth shattering, but it was enough to prove to me that my career in tech wasn't over. In fact, it was only just beginning. I had just graduated from what should have been the first stage in any tech career: Failure Boot Camp.

THE INVESTMENT FALLACY REVISITED

There are great venture capitalists out there. And there are great incubators and opportunities for startups and founders that didn't exist five years ago, let alone a decade, or a generation, ago. But this improved environment for startups has fostered a fallacy that can be debilitating for individual startups and detrimental to the scene as a whole: the belief that raising investment is a mark of success and that it increases the likelihood of you, the founder, ultimately getting a return on your business. This belief is false.

Venture capital is a core feature of the startup world, yet how it actually works is not well known. So it's worth probing into it a little deeper here.

I didn't fully learn this myself until I became a VC. I worked as a venture partner for a $1 billion venture capital fund. Subsequently, as an angel investor, I have invested in over forty companies.

Angel investors are a little different: they invest their own money. Apart from the angels, the money a VC invests normally isn't his own—it comes from his investors. Investors typically come from among the world's elite: family offices, endowments, sovereign wealth funds. These have billions of dollars sitting around, and they are risk averse: their goal, simply, is to not lose it.

So they spread their money all over the globe, in every type of opportunity, in order to hedge against the risk of losses: a recession in one area or meltdown in one industry may cause losses to a part of their portfolios, but these are likely to be offset by gains elsewhere.

How this works in the tech sector is a little different. VCs that invest in tech don't do so on the basis of careful hedging of investments to ensure steady single-digit growth. Instead, they hope for massive gains on a very small proportion of their investments.

That the remainder will fail is incidental. Low-level success is largely irrelevant. They expect that most of the eggs in their basket will break: six or seven out of ten of their investments will be write-offs; another two or three will be base hits; one in ten will make a tenfold return. That's the one they're waiting for. That's what they need in order to compensate for the other failures.

But that's not what a founder necessarily needs.

Recently, a friend called me for advice. He is a CEO and founder, and a large competitor had approached him with an offer to acquire his company for $15 million. He has a one-third share, so he would pocket $5 million from the deal.

He is recently married and still carrying debts from years of struggle to bring this company to life. Five million dollars would be life changing.

But he is under pressure from his investors not to take it. His largest investor bought a third of the business the previous year at a $12 million valuation. He stands to make $1 million on a $4 million investment—a 25 percent return.

That may seem like a reasonable return, but VCs typically aren't interested in reasonable returns. They are looking for the one in ten that will make a tenfold return. My friend's VC investor would rather my friend hold on in pursuit of that outcome than take the money on offer and exit now.

The emotional and financial pressure that VC can bring to bear is likely to mean that my friend will turn down the offer, which could be the biggest mistake of his life.

To appreciate the significance of this, place yourself in his shoes, but imagine you also have $5 million in savings. Refusing an acquisition that will net you $5 million is exactly the same in effect as taking your entire $5 million savings and investing it in the business. In each case, $5 million in cash is being forsaken in the (very uncertain) hope of a greater future payoff.

That's the kind of decision that VCs make on behalf of their super wealthy investors. And it's a decision that can be entirely at odds with the interests of the founder.

That is one way in which the interests of investors may not be aligned with those of the founder's. But in the case of my games studio, we were out of sync in more basic ways.

When I took on the role of CEO, I hadn't realized that there was a whole new role of investor relations that needed to be performed. I didn't realize that I needed to manage my shareholders on top of all the other management challenges.

I already had a debt (of honor as well as money) to the first-round investors, so I was desperate to keep the company—and hence the dream—alive. But I failed to realize that with that money came the responsibility of managing those investors' expectations.

With investors, when you don't talk to them, they assume everything's going great. The longer you don't talk to them, the greater they think things are going.

But as time went on and their expectations went up, my ability to execute went down. This mismatch was a time bomb. I allowed it to go so far that eventually it exploded.

If your startup *clearly* needs an investment in order to reach its market, then you are entitled to take some satisfaction from successfully raising that investment. But this satisfaction should be tempered by the understanding that you must now achieve much more than you previously needed to, and, even as you concentrate on that management challenge, you must manage your investors' expectations.

Investment success tells you nothing about whether you can deliver on your vision, get that vision into the market, or if the market will appreciate it. The chief thing that investment success gives you is an extra burden of responsibility on your shoulders.

The minute you raise money, any future exit has to pay back that investment in order to be considered a success. The more money you take, the more you have to pay back: investment is basically debt. Henceforth, your investors will review all of your major strategic decisions in an exclusively profit-oriented environment—investors aren't in it for the creative kick.

Just getting to that exit is hard enough on its own without the burden of increased expectations. As I learned, it requires time spent *communicating* as well as simply *doing*—and time may be as precious a resource, or more precious, than the funding you raised.

I took investment. I didn't fully understand the consequences. And I paid for it.

TAKEAWAY: HOW TO AVOID THE INVESTMENT FALLACY

- Ignore your team, the tech press, the cheerleaders: when you get a decent investment offer, they will all tell you to accept it.
- The longer you can hold out without investment, the greater your control, the greater the ultimate rewards, and the greater your chance of success.
- If you must take investment, remember: the job now gets harder, not easier. Don't party: get back to work.

FALLACY FOUR: THE "FAILURE IS NOT AN OPTION" FALLACY

THE "FAILURE IS NOT AN OPTION" FALLACY

(AND HOW I LEARNED TO FAIL BETTER)

> *Do. Or do not. There is no try.*
> *–Yoda*

> *Winners never quit, and quitters never win.*
> *–Ted Turner*

"TRYING" IS FOR LOSERS. *Visionaries, leaders, founders—these are not the kind of people who try—these are people who win. The winner mentality brooks no compromise—there is no room in it for thought of failure.*

That was how I approached my first businesses too. But by my mid-twenties, I had already failed multiple times.

"Failure is not an option" is one of the most beloved mantras of gurus everywhere. It is a fallacy. Failure is not a choice: it is an outcome. That outcome may come about as a result of your mistakes; or it may come about as a result of events outside your control. Either way, making the right choices about how to handle that failure is a crucial step to ultimate business success.

The trick is not to act like failure is not *an option—the trick is to know when failure is* the right *option.*

I had yet to have a success—but, with my next startup, I had my first "good" failure.

HOW I LEARNED TO FAIL BETTER

Someday, perhaps you'll sit with a grandchild on your lap, and he or she will turn to you and say, "Grandpa/Grandma, tell me your story about 'letters' again."

And you'll explain how, when you were young, if you wanted to send an important message to someone, you wrote or printed it on paper, and then you put the paper in an envelope, wrote where the person lived on the envelope, licked a stamp, and put the stamp on the envelope.

Then you walked to a post box to post it so that it would arrive at the address a few days later. And then, after a few days had passed, you phoned the person to make sure the letter had been received...

FOR A WHILE AFTER I CRASHED AND BURNED on the games studio and sports dot-com, I worked as a freelance consultant, taking tech work on retainer while concentrating on other areas of my life (such as my growing family). I had various low-value software maintenance contracts that were easy to fulfill and provided a reasonable revenue stream.

To keep this revenue flowing, all I needed to do was to keep my cell phone handy, check e-mail regularly, and, of course, invoice my clients. But I found the supposedly straightforward business of printing and sending invoices to be bewilderingly difficult.

I had no difficulty keeping clients' websites ticking over, responding promptly to queries, and keeping in good contact with them. But I consistently managed to mess up my invoicing.

The problem wasn't so much the accountancy side of it as the logistics. The simple acts of keeping a stock of paper, envelopes, print cartridges, and stamps and then making the short journey to post the invoices repeatedly defeated me.

This became such a headache that I found myself putting off doing my invoices. And that led to the sums building up and my accounts becoming more complicated, and me putting them off further.

This was a vital part of my business, and I was doing it badly. And I was getting far more stressed about the stamps and envelopes bit than I was about the consultancy work. But there wasn't enough of this secretarial work to justify hiring somebody to do it for me. And then, as I fumbled for an envelope in my office in the early hours of one morning, I knew exactly what I needed. I needed a computer to do it for me.

I wanted it to be as easy as two clicks—like printing. You open the Print menu and click Print. So you should open the Post menu and click Post.

With that command, your computer would tell some service somewhere to print your document, address an envelope, insert the document into the envelope, lick the stamp, put it on the envelope, and post it—ASAP.

Then I realized something: all the technology already existed to do this. It would be relatively simple, although not without some potentially satisfying technical challenges. And if I felt the need for such a service, there must be others who did too.

I dug two old Linux Pentium machines out of storage. They were relics, but they still had plenty of firepower to run the website and servers. I spent $4,500 on a secondhand Hewlett Packard 5200MP printer. And I went to work on the programming.

It took me about forty-eight sleepless hours to hack through the initial documentation, code samples, and missed approaches. By then I had a proof of concept that clearly demonstrated I could deliver on the idea: an automated postal service. It was clunky, but it told me the concept was worth running with—technically, at least. This part of the process was exhilarating. It may be a tiny innovation in the broader scheme of things, but out of six billion souls on this planet, I knew that at that moment I was the only one utilizing technology in precisely that way to create a new technological function.

This felt revolutionary. In some tiny way, my invention could change the lives of some tiny portion of the human population.

It could make their working lives more efficient and more satisfying. And who knows what benefits could flow from that?

Though a key lesson in this book is to avoid being seduced by this process (see Fallacies One and Ten), for me, *at root*, technology is about creating things that are unique and beautiful. It is an art and, at this stage in creating it, at least, we are artists. Now that I had a working concept, I started working toward engagement with the market. I registered domain names, hired designers to build an identity, and wrote content to clarify the vision. I called the product PostASAP.

Within a couple of months of my eureka moment, I had a product ready to launch. But what next? How do you get a product into the market? What do you *charge* for it?

You might think I'd have thought of that earlier. I'd built a new product for a market I had *assumed* was out there, but the extent of my market research had consisted of me sitting alone in my office, late at night, failing to find stamps. I had a test market sample size of one.

I reached out to Michael Crandell, who had successfully exited from his startup, eFax. Crandell advised me to use varying landing pages for PostASAP, with different subscription and prepaid options, and to use Google Ads to direct people to them.

He may not have realized it, but Crandell gave me a tool for how to evaluate whether the business was going to be successful, not merely how much to charge for it. This simple insight turned out to be the seed of an entrepreneur superpower—I continue to draw on it today. (I'll explain how in Fallacy Nine.)

Within sixty days, we had 340 sign-ups. Eighty-six customers had given up their credit card details (the rest were still within the trial period, or had signed up on one of the landing pages that offered free usage). Those eighty-six were being billed $5 each per month, meaning we were taking in a total of $450 per month and each customer was likely to earn us $90 over an estimated eighteen-month lifetime with us.

The problem was the cost of acquiring those customers. We were paying Google an average of ten cents per click for Google Ads. But our conversion rate—the number of visitors to our site who subsequently paid for the service—was tiny.

It took almost five thousand clicks at ten cents per click to get a paying customer—a cost of $500 per customer—a customer who would only return $90 to us if he or she stayed with us for a year and a half.

Crandell gave us a formula that seemed obvious in hindsight but that, at the time, was revelatory in its simplicity and brute logic:

The money you'll make over the lifetime of your customer less the cost to acquire that customer has to be positive or you aren't viable.

We were spending $500 to make $90. We weren't viable.

This was a shock to me. I *knew* how valuable this service was—because it had sprung from my own business needs. It was genuinely innovative and filled a demonstrable niche in the market. But the problem was simple: people weren't ready to pay for it.

PostASAP had no immediate competitors with which customers could compare pricing. So what would they compare our pricing with? With the *existing* technology. And what was the existing technology? The postal service.

The postal service may be cumbersome, but it is cheap. And it is deeply culturally embedded. When people think of the cost of sending a letter, they merely think of the cost of the stamp, even though there are, of course, additional monetary and time costs involved.

So, when they checked out our PostASAP service, the only mental guide they had for what it should cost was the price of a stamp. Of course, had they considered the time involved in getting the invoice into the post, and the costs involved when invoices are delayed (or even forgotten) because of the hassle of physically posting them, they would have realized the opportunity cost to them was far higher than the difference between our service and the price of a stamp. But this required an imaginative leap; if they didn't make it, PostASAP would seem ridiculously overpriced.

So I had another notch on my failure belt. This time, though, I would handle that failure much better. I may not have made progress in pure business terms, but I had made crucial progress as an entrepreneur: I had learned how to fail.

THE TECH FALLACY *AGAIN*

When a mathematician stumbles upon an unsolved problem, she feels a nagging pressure grow in the back of her brain that relentlessly pushes her to seek a solution. When a sculptor has a vision for a block of marble, he has to excavate it until that vision is brought to life. The entrepreneur has a similar reaction when stumbling upon a new business idea. It must be acted on!

This was how I felt when I had that eureka moment in my office late at night while fumbling for an envelope and stamps. This is how I built most of my early products, and it's how most founders who pitch me for investment have created their products.

This is the Tech Fallacy in operation again. It is perhaps the most pervasive of these fallacies because it draws on something instinctive in many of us: the desire to create good tech.

The harsh lesson I was to learn, yet again, with Post-ASAP was that the tech isn't enough. If the market isn't there, the tech is pointless.

This makes it crucial to start thinking about the market as soon as you conceive of a product. You may have discovered an elegant and economic solution to a problem, but is there a market for resolving that problem?

There may be a niche in the market, but is there a market in the niche?

THE "FAILURE IS NOT AN OPTION" FALLACY REVISITED

The younger me would have persisted with PostASAP past the point where it looked unviable, fighting to the last to make it work. I would have burned friends and investors—and, ultimately, burned out—to make it work.

But I had learned from previous failures and had the experience of Michael Crandell to draw on also. I was determined to avoid the kind of chaotic, ugly collapse that I had been through previously.

This time, I saw the writing on the wall and took preemptive action. I shut down PostASAP—but with a plan for what would follow.

The idea of preparing for failure, as a founder, appears contradictory. How can you possibly succeed if you're preparing to fail?

But the industry knows that most startups fail. Investors know— they *expect*—that most startups they invest in will fail. Smart founders *should* know the environment they're working in, and they should know that, no matter how good their idea or how hard they work, the odds of success are stacked against them.

All startup founders need a failure plan: a plan for how to identify *when* your company has failed, *what* to do to shut it down, and *how* to do it. *Who* do you go to? *How much* does it cost? (Yes, closing a company *costs money*.) What sort of severance and notice for staff do you need to budget for?

The failure plan should contain automatic triggers for when you should activate the plan (or at least consider it). The point of this is to make the decision to activate the plan—i.e., to shut down the company—as clinical and automatic as possible in order to remove the risk of being blinded by passion or fear.

You should write down the plan and share it with the team and investors. Once the triggers are reached, the failure plan should kick in. The company will get wound up as efficiently and as fairly as possible, there will be minimal collateral damage and—crucially—you, the founder, will be free to rebound quickly onto the next project.

The crux of the failure plan for PostASAP was this: if we discover that the cost to acquire customers is greater than the amount we can make from them, let's not do the business.

The one thing we could have done to reach the point where we could evaluate that quicker would have been to not build the tech in the first place: to have tested the offering by giving people the opportunity to sign up for a service not yet developed.

After all, the failure plan did not require that a customer actually *use* the product. We could have launched a website with stated pricing and still have measured the conversion rate of those customers, even if the product itself hadn't existed. This is now my entrepreneur "superpower"—despite how simple and obvious it may seem, it took me years to embrace it in practice. (See Fallacy Nine.)

SO I HAD CHALKED UP ANOTHER FAILURE. But, this time, there were no threats that I'd never work in tech again. The question was what next?

Though PostASAP's pricing model failed, I noticed that most of those subscribers who stayed with it after initially trying it out were using it for the precise function I had in mind when I initially conceived of it: to issue invoices.

There may not have been a market for a generic online postal service, but it seemed there could be one for an online invoicing service. As I put the failure plan for PostASAP into action, I started to conceive of a successor: it would be called BillASAP.

My failure plan had minimized the collateral damage from the failure of PostASAP. I had a strong team who had remained loyal. I had a good idea and, after learning from past mistakes, I had a determination to test it on the market experts. I was determined that this next project would work.

TAKEAWAY: HOW TO AVOID THE "FAILURE IS NOT AN OPTION" FALLACY

- Plan for failure. Don't expect *to* fail—but do expect *that you might* fail.
- Learn about the process of closing down a business: how to do it fairly and efficiently. Set negative targets: if you hit these, despite your best efforts, then you automatically trigger your failure plan and start winding down the company.
- Failing this way means you're more likely to retain the loyalty of your colleagues and the respect of your clients and customers. And that makes you more likely to bounce back and succeed the next time.

FAILURE BOOT CAMP

Incubators, universities, mentors, and business-development programs all offer advice and instruction on how to succeed with your business. But no one teaches you how to fail.

This is a glaring oversight. Fail badly, and you may be truly finished. Fail well, and you can take the best of your experience with you—the learning, the contacts, the ideas—and start again.

This is why there's an urgent need for a "failure boot camp." This would teach you to make your own bespoke failure *plan*—a plan for how to identify when your company has failed and what to do to shut it down.

Having a failure plan makes you no more likely to fail than having safety drills makes commercial airlines more likely to crash. You're not *planning* to fail; you're planning what to do *if* you fail.

The games studio became my failure boot camp (see Fallacy Three); but it would have been easier to learn those lessons in an actual camp.

The key lesson I took from it was this:

It's not the failing that really hurts. It's the stuff you do in your bid to avoid recognizing *the failure that has already happened* that really hurts.

FALLACY FIVE: THE EXPERT FALLACY

THE EXPERT FALLACY

(AND HOW I LEARNED FROM MY PAST AND MISSED THE FUTURE)

"The experts know best."

ASKING AN EXPERT IS A GOOD IDEA... *if you're digging the foundations for a house, if your engine won't start, if you've got green spots on your tongue.*

But if you're building an innovative start-up targeting non-expert users, the "experts" are the last people you want to talk to.

The Expert Fallacy is the belief that the experts know best. In startup culture, the Expert Fallacy leads many a founder to rely on the analysis of established experts when, by definition, nobody can be an expert in a new product, service or market.

You do need to learn from the experience of others. You do need to take good advice. You do need to study your field. But there's a time and a place for experts. Choosing that time and place—and being ready to disregard the experts outside of that—is a hard-won skill As I learned on my next startup.

HOW I LEARNED FROM MY PAST AND MISSED THE FUTURE

It's one am. I don't know when I last slept. We're launching tomorrow. We've been working toward this launch for nine months—or eighteen if you count the previous failed project that directly led to this one. The six of us on the team have been living and working in my shed. My family is at just the other end of the garden but for weeks I've hardly seen them. There are pizza boxes and Coke cans strewn everywhere. The air is stale. There is a permanent hum from overworked PCs. We've put a quarter of a million dollars in time and money into this. By the end of tomorrow, this product should be worth double that.

Then my chief technical officer, buried in his screen, calls me - a note of panic in his voice. "I think you should see this."

All six of us gather around his screen. On it is a mirror image of our product—except better. A rival is offering a similar product to ours—a product we thought was going to be unique. A product we thought was going to disrupt the market. A competitor we didn't even know about has beaten us to it.

Not only have they beaten us on speed, they have beaten us on execution too. It is immediately clear that they are streets ahead of us—so far ahead that their presence changes the nature of the market. We can't compete.

My mouth is dry, my head fuzzy. Weeks of too little sleep have suddenly caught up with me. The clarity of thought and purpose that has driven me through this last hectic, climactic stage is gone. In its place is an insistent thudding inside the front of my skull, just above my right temple. I slump back into my chair; the screen in front of me is an irrelevant haze. I barely recognize the imagery on it—imagery to which I was fervently making last-minute adjustments just minutes before.

"J, we need to make a call," says the CTO. "What do you think?"

What do I think? I *can't* think.

"What's in your gut?" he asks.

That is simpler. I know how I *feel*.

"We're fucked."

So there will be no launch tomorrow. There will be no product. There may not even be a company, depending on what each of the team members decides to do. How did this happen? How could we have gotten it so wrong?

We had asked the experts.

WHEN WE TOOK A HARD LOOK AT WHAT COULD BE SALVAGED from PostASAP, we realized that our most loyal customers were all using it for invoicing. Small businesses found invoicing to be an inefficient and cumbersome chore, but when they put it off, or did it haphazardly, they were disproportionately punished.

Invoicing, by definition, is not core business, and yet it is a crucial business function. What small businesses needed was a way to outsource their invoicing. And because the consequence of improving their efficiency in this department would be so immediately obvious—quicker and more reliable invoices means quicker and more reliable payment—they would, I thought, be willing to pay for the service.

PostASAP wasn't viable because people instinctively compared the cost of the service to the cost of a stamp. But with an invoicing service, I thought they might compare the cost of the service to the return from the invoice. With the cost of sending an invoice merely the tiniest fraction of the value of that invoice, outsourced invoicing was a service, I believed, that could readily be monetized.

We developed a simple demo to send online invoices and called it BillASAP. Then we sought feedback. Logically, we went to the people most familiar with the task at hand: those accountants and bookkeepers already using complex existing software packages to do their invoicing.

They asked us, where was per-line-item tax? Shipping versus billing addresses? Billing terms? Multiple customer contacts? Multiple projects per account? Line-item quantities? Invoice details with account balances? Searchable fields? Recurring invoices? Templates? Where was QuickBooks integration?

And so, building on their insights, we built an online competitor to the market leader, QuickBooks, which provided accountancy software to small businesses.

Had I been following my own, hard-won, earlier insights, I would have done just the design and marketing before doing any programing. But I'm a programmer at heart, and I had found a problem I could sink my teeth into; I wasn't going to let go till I had fully digested it. Does that sound familiar? It's the Tech Fallacy *again*—once again, I was mired in it.

And so we built the product, convinced that there was a market for it simply by our own enthusiasm for it.

Had we tested that market, we would have realized:

(a) there was already a competitor in that space, and

(b) what that competitor was providing, and what the market now wanted, was not what the "experts" prescribed, but something very different – something simple and quicker.

We were giving them a fully-specced MP3 player – but the market wanted the iPod Shuffle.

THE EXPERT FALLACY REVISITED

I'm reluctant to make a guru of Donald Rumsfeld. But for this, I'll make an exception.

There are known knowns; there are things we know we know. We also know there are known unknowns; that is to say we know there are some things we do not know. But there are also unknown unknowns—the ones we don't know we don't know.
– Donald Rumsfeld, 2002

This is a key concept in epistemology, the philosophy of knowledge. Breaking it down, it suggests there are three types of knowledge:

- Things you know
- Things you know you don't know
- Things you *don't* know you don't know.

After failing with PostASAP, there were things *we knew we knew*. We knew how to build the technology to automate a print-and-post service. We knew we needed to attack a big market that was willing to spend money. And we knew from PostASAP that there were small businesses wanting to ease the pain of invoicing.

We also *knew* that we *didn't know* certain things. We didn't know how much it would cost to acquire users. We didn't know the price point at which we could attract users.

We didn't know whether there was a market of users who were ready to do their invoicing online: did enough companies have sufficiently reliable Internet to do all their invoicing online? (This was 2006—a different age as far as the Internet was concerned. Broadband penetration was still far from complete.)

And would they trust another company with this most sensitive of business information?

But there were also *unknown unknowns*—things we *didn't know* we *didn't know*.

In retrospect, the key unknown unknown was that the Internet was going through a subtle but significant evolution. Till then, software applications were traditionally installed on the individual user's computer. But around this time, software started migrating to the Internet.

This evolutionary moment was recognized and labeled "Web 2.0" for a while, but the term quickly began to grate. Now, we know its core innovation as "software-as-a-service" (SaaS).

This move from hosting software on individual computers to hosting it in the cloud enabled a new set of users to access software previously accessibly only to larger and wealthier organizations. The subscription model enabled users to pay modest monthly fees instead of prohibitive up-front charges.

Accompanying this change in delivery and pricing was a change in style. There was a new focus on the user experience and on simplicity. Instead of feature-rich websites mimicking the complexity of desktop software, a new breed of websites stripped their services back to their core value, their unique selling point: the simplest way to get what you needed done. This, in turn, made them accessible to much larger markets.

Key business services were on the front lines of this movement. The software market for project management, invoicing, estimating, bookkeeping, and human resources services was dominated by bulky, expensive software packages. Not only were they expensive, but they were complex. Small businesses would have to hire a specialist to run them, or train up a team member.

Take the field of project management, for example. To create a project plan in the leading project management software, Microsoft Project, you had to answer questions on dependencies, resource allocations, critical paths, and Gantt charts. Then along came an upstart, Basecamp.

com. Its premise was laughable: it was just an online checklist.

It turned out this was just what many people needed. They didn't want other features—or the burden of learning how to use them, or the pricing. This super simple hook launched a major new business that fast became a market leader. (Basecamp's founders, 37Signals, subsequently published a series of influential management books.)

No expert would have advised aspiring project management software makers to develop a *checklist*. And our experts advised us to abandon simple invoicing and develop precisely the same intimidating complexity that was keeping our target user away from the existing software.

The experts know how things traditionally work better than anyone else does, but when markets are changing, their perspective can be misleading. The experts have bought into the existing system more than other people have. Experts can't see the need for a market move in the first place. They assume the premises of the existing market so strongly that they often don't understand the need for change.

My father was a case in point: having trained for years to become a nuclear safety specialist, it took him years to realize that the very thing he was a specialist in – nuclear accidents – was the thing that would destroy the market for his services .

The new market didn't want a complex software package. The new market had no bias toward what was already existing. It just needed a critical business task done. And the simpler the better.

Our online invoicing rival—a company called Blinksale—understood this intuitively. The difference between their offering and ours was so stark, it seemed revolutionary. (Like all such revolutions, it seems obvious in retrospect.)

We were positioning ourselves as an online competitor to the offline market leader, QuickBooks. But Blinksale's attitude was: What's the market?

We were trying to appeal to an audience that would never have come to us. We were going after QuickBooks aficionados, but by definition, QuickBooks aficionados were conservative. Blinksale was going after the market that was repelled by QuickBooks—and the market that didn't even know QuickBooks existed. They were redefining the market.

This was another "unknown unknown" that we faced. In retrospect, it was embarrassingly obvious. We didn't know *who our market was*, and, therefore, we didn't know what they wanted. And we *didn't know* that we didn't know this, because we were relying on insights gained through developing an earlier product, not through rigorous testing of the new market.

We had simply trusted that by providing a better service than an existing one, users would migrate to us. It hadn't occurred to us that those users might be too loyal to their existing service to move.

And if we couldn't find our market among existing users of invoicing software, where would we find it? Among people who had *never used* invoicing software.

Again, that answer seems obvious in retrospect, but because we didn't think of the *question*, we never thought to look for the answer.

Despite the hours and money we had invested in BillASAP, the decision to pull it wasn't difficult. There was no choice. Not only would Blinksale have likely beaten us in the market, but to compete in the first place, we would have had to defend an inferior, misguided product. That wasn't us. Our hearts weren't in it.

The Expert Fallacy is deeply ingrained in our culture, not merely in the tech sector. It's the belief that the expert knows best.

Experts are good when you want to know how something works. But when you want to challenge the very premise of something, experts are the last people you should talk to.

Their expertise roots them even more firmly than most in the systems within which they work. They have invested more in them and are more committed to them. So when you want to challenge those systems, you can't rely on the experts.

The classic case of the Expert Fallacy occurred in the development of digital photography. Back in 2000, the industry belief was that the market wanted digital cameras that were feature rich and of ever-improving quality.

The camera phone turned that on its head. It turned out that the market wanted greater ease of use and convenience, and was happy to accept worse quality.

The iPod is another example. Steve Jobs took the MP3 player *backward* with the release of the iPod Shuffle. By stripping out features and focusing on simplicity, he created a new market.

The subprime mortgage crisis was another, more catastrophic example. As Michael Lewis details in his book *The Big Short*, the experts all believed that the financial system had rigorous risk architecture in place and failed to see that this was built on sand. The people who spotted this were mostly outsiders and mavericks.

Blinksale provided me with a massive wake-up call. I was so embedded in my industry niche that it took a dramatic defeat to show me that there was a different way of bringing applications to market. To all of us, that night in my shed, it was clear that Blinksale heralded a revolution for how we, at least, would henceforth develop applications. The core value would be simplicity.

We didn't break to drown our sorrows. Blinksale slapped us across the face, but as much as it stung, it was invigorating. Those guys, we realized, with growing excitement, were on to something.

They had insights we could use and strengths we could learn from. That night, we set about learning precisely how Blinksale outperformed BillASAP, with the intuition that the insight gleaned would drive our next project.

If you're trying to do something new, you can't sell it to the people who want the old. For new products, you need new markets.

TAKEAWAY: HOW TO AVOID THE EXPERT FALLACY

- Beware of the experts. Don't ignore them altogether, but look to them for targeted expertise, not systemic analysis. Experts, by definition, have bought into the system. If you want to create systemic change, they won't help you.

KNOWNS & UNKNOWNS: A RUMSFELDIAN APPROACH TO BUSINESS PLANNING

Had I applied Donald Rumsfeld's insight to the planning of BillASAP, I might have written a memo like this.

Knowns:
- We can build the technology.
- We need to attack a market that is willing to spend money.
- Small businesses need a service like this.

Known Unknowns
- How much will it cost to acquire users?
- At what price point will users sign up?
- Are sufficient numbers of users ready to use this service online?
- Will they trust a third party with such sensitive information?

Unknown Unknowns (revealed with hindsight):
- The mode of delivery of software will change, from desktop installation to cloud-based subscriptions.
- This change will create an entirely new market that will demand different things of core services (most notably, simplicity).

FALLACY SIX: THE IDEA FALLACY

a draft business presentation. I called Kevin and told him to come round.

"Holy shit," he said, "you already built it!"

And we had. It was crude and ungainly, but it was there: a personalized shopping cart for the web. Kevin came on board officially, and we worked hell for leather to get it to market. For six weeks, I slept two hours a night; most of the rest was spent in the shed, barring a few hours a day with my family. By the end of that period, we were ready to test it. We called it RightCart.

Within weeks, it had been written up on TechCrunch and was installed on tens of thousands of sites. Individual carts had had millions of views.

And so, finally—after multiple failures—I had a success. And then the VCs came calling.

RightCart's ethos of making selling and shopping easier—of *democratizing* e-commerce—was in tune with the zeitgeist.

But the VCs wanted me to tell a more dramatic story—one of revolutionary proportions. The VCs wanted me to talk of "social web e-commerce." In this brave new world, they said, every blogger would be a business. This, they said, would make RightCart a multimillion-dollar company.

I didn't believe them. I had wanted to improve the online shopping experience. I had no interest in creating and running a social media widget company. So instead of courting the VCs, I did a tour of company boardrooms.

I visited Visa, Amazon, Buy.com, Adbrite, and others. I was touting my company, but I was also using it to get inside those rooms and to gain contacts and insights into how the market leaders ran their businesses.

With the VCs whispering promises of multimillions in my ear, I took an offer of $250,000 from Buy.com.

It had cost me $120,000 and six months to develop RightCart. (Although I could argue that it had taken two years, given that the PostASAP and BillASAP failures were effectively part of the "development" process.) To the market, and my startup peers, $250,000 was not a dramatic exit.

Modest though this success may have been, it was efficient, and it was exhilarating. It gave me some financial freedom to take risks with new products, and it gave me the confidence to back myself in doing so.

It was, finally, a validation from the market (not merely from investors). It was also, of course, a validation of Kevin Milden's idea. But the fact that the original idea was not mine in no way lessened my sense of achievement.

Had Kevin wanted to, he could have developed the product himself. He was generous in sharing the idea, but he also knew that he wasn't going to develop it.

A less mature entrepreneur would have clutched that idea selfishly to himself, jealous of the hypothetical success anybody else might have with it. But Kevin understood that the tech ecosystem relies on cooperation and collaboration. Good ideas well executed make everybody's lives better. Good ideas kept secret add nothing to the world.

THE IDEA FALLACY REVISITED

During the dot-com boom, in 2001, it seemed like anyone with a half-baked idea for a dot-com had money thrown at them.

This was the epitome of the Idea Fallacy: "It's all about the idea," the VCs screamed and the media chorused; the would-be founders soaked it up and were duly soaked in cash, no matter that many of them lacked so badly in the ability to execute.

Websites for selling pet supplies (pets.com) and groceries (Webvan) attracted hundreds of millions of dollars in venture capital almost overnight and then went spectacularly bust because their models were chronically unprofitable. Webvan, for example, had raised $800 million and taken thirty-year leases on warehouses, only to find that its core business of grocery deliveries didn't work in the market.

Then came the backlash: following the bursting of the dot-com bubble, the market swung back to place new emphasis on execution. This helped foster the excesses of the Tech Fallacy, where investors encouraged techies to play to their instinctive bias and focus on the tech to the exclusion of all else.

These things move in cycles. Still, the Idea Fallacy remains pervasive. That's because it is at the heart of contemporary popular culture, not merely the tech sector.

Every time someone looks at a work of art and says, "I could have done that if I'd thought of it," that's the Idea Fallacy at work. Every time somebody reads about Mark Zuckerberg or Jack Dorsey or Larry Page or Sergey Brin and thinks, "Lucky bastard. I wish I'd thought of that," that's the Idea Fallacy again.

The Idea Fallacy is the belief that *inspiration*, not *perspiration*, is the fount of creative success, whether in the arts, the creative industries, or in startups. It is the belief that the root of success lies in the idea rather than the execution—the belief that ideas have substantial intrinsic value—that they are the key item in the startup value chain.

Not only was RightCart not my idea, it wasn't even a new idea at all. Shopping carts were everywhere. There were even preexisting shopping carts that would follow you around the web: Yahoo Stores, Shopify, and others.

What distinguished us was near-perfect execution. We chose the right technology. We had a beautiful design. We came to market fast—with what I would come to think of as a "minimum viable product" (which I'll talk more about in Fallacy Nine). We invested barely anything in the product (in time or money) till we had market feedback. We had a good PR story. We took our exit at our very first opportunity.

Rarely is an idea original. Society's focus on the "Big Idea" is misplaced. As Jim Collins shows in *Great by Choice*, many of our business icons build their success on the back of other people's ideas: it wasn't the McDonald brothers who built McDonald's into an empire, it was Ray Kroc who saw the seed of greater success in their operation and bought it from them.

Southwest Airlines copied its model directly from Pacific Southwest Airlines. Ryanair, Europe's largest airline—named after one of its founders, Tony Ryan—was a loss-making tiny Irish airline until Michael O'Leary applied the Southwest model and duly revolutionized the European airline industry.

Facebook, Google, Apple, Uber, Airbnb, Zappos—none of them were built on original ideas. Competitors were doing the same thing at the same time, sometimes even before them. But they executed better.

The Idea Fallacy warns us not to be seduced by the brilliance of our ideas—an idea without execution is worthless. But it also tells us not to be intimidated by the fact that others may already be executing the same idea.

This is counterintuitive to many first-time founders. Let's say you have what you think is a brilliant business idea and you want to see if it's viable. Which of these situations would you prefer to find?

a. There are existing businesses with the same idea that are thriving.
b. There are existing businesses with the same idea that are struggling.
c. There are no businesses with that idea.

First-time founders always answer (c). For me, the answer is always (a).

One of the first challenges a startup faces is to prove that there is a market for its product. The existence of thriving competitors proves that there is a market. After that, it's all about *execution*: if you execute better than the competitors, you will win market share.

If, instead, there are competitors but they are struggling, that may be because they were seduced by their idea and failed to realize that there were intrinsic obstacles to executing it. It may mean the market is inadequate.

If there are no businesses with that idea, then perhaps there is simply no market for it—no matter how brilliant you think it is.

I face this as an investor all the time. Give me nine founders with amazing ideas but minimal execution abilities and one founder with proven execution ability but a bland and predictable idea, and I'll go for the latter every time.

TAKEAWAY: HOW TO AVOID THE IDEA FALLACY

- Don't be seduced by the brilliance of your idea—or anybody else's. Test it on the market: if it works, develop it. If it doesn't, move on. If there are already competitors with the same idea and they're thriving, that proves there's a market. Take it on.
- Share your ideas—don't hoard them. An idea that you're never going to execute could be the seed of somebody else's success—and help make the ecosystem better for everyone.

FALLACY SEVEN: THE SCALE FALLACY

THE SCALE FALLACY

(AND HOW I LEARNED THE VALUE OF SUCCESS THAT WAS STEADY, NOT SPECTACULAR)

"There's no value in services, because they don't scale."

STARTUP CULTURE SAYS THAT SUCCESS MUST BE SCALABLE: *growth should be "exponential"; distribution should be "viral." This makes services the poor cousin in the startup world.*

Services businesses don't tell the story of spectacular success that VCs and the media want. By definition, they are limited in scale to the number of personnel. Services are not a quick way to fame, glory, and riches.

But services can be a crucial facilitator of startup success. They can be the bedrock on which a founder's career is built. And, though they may never make you a billionaire, they can bring great rewards nonetheless: they can bring you into creative, corporate, and social spaces to which you'd never otherwise have had access.

The Scale Fallacy convinces would-be founders to focus on digital products that scale. But focusing on the services they could sell would make many of them more successful more quickly, and that might give them a platform on which to later build a scalable startup.

HOW I LEARNED THE VALUE OF SUCCESS THAT WAS STEADY, NOT SPECTACULAR

As I lurched from startup failure to failure, I had a safety net that caught me and helped me rebound each time. It ensured my failure never wiped me out, that I had a team of colleagues to support me, and that I had a regular income. It gave me access to the executives and boardrooms of leading companies and insight into changes in the market and technology.

This safety net was a consultancy. Even as I relentlessly pursued the founder dream, I was never afraid to dial for dollars. From the age of fourteen, I consistently sold my services. I started out helping friends' parents buy their first PCs and then graduated to providing tech installation and maintenance services to local businesses. After college, alongside running a startup games studio, I founded a consultancy to trade on the skills of my team. Unusual for the times, we had core technical skills. We were willing to work on other people's projects on the side and so quickly found ourselves in demand as consultants.

This was the era of the Idea Fallacy: many of those projects were nothing more than an idea; their promoters placed little to no emphasis on execution and often had no technical skills – despite being supposed "tech startups."

One such startup was ForewardLinks.com. They proposed to build a website to schedule tee times at golf courses and raised $5 million dollars. They hired us to build it, which we duly did. But there was a slight problem: few golf courses in those days had Internet connections. ForwardLinks.com tanked soon after.

As we learned from our own failures, as well as those of others, and took on board the coding language Ruby and the agile development process, we became a team of consultant-innovators, building new products for other people to bring to market.

The era changed. The sector learned (so it thought) from the excesses of the dot-com bubble, follies such as pets.com, Webvan, and, on a smaller scale, ForwardLinks.com. Investors saw the fallacy of the exclusive emphasis on ideas and sought to place new emphasis on the tech. They came to us for that expertise.

But, for most, there was still a crucial piece missing: bringing the product to market.

"Will it scale?" a client would ask as we talked them through the development process.

"What scale do you need?" I'd ask.

"A million users a day."

We could build that without difficulty. But they were usually lucky to get a hundred users a day. Those clients were focusing on the *product*, as if that were the hard part of the development process. I learned from watching them fail that *going to market* was the hard part.

One such project was a piece of mobile phone software for going to Disney World. We built it rich with beautiful detail, such as graphics of tiny roller coasters on a map. But the client hadn't tested the market…

It turned out that the market didn't exist. Disney owned the relevant intellectual property and wasn't about to share it. So our beautiful piece of software went straight in the bin.

Watching client after client repeat these mistakes, I started to change the way we built products for clients. I would make them do a "mini" project—a rough prototype, a kind of minimum viable product—in order to get feedback early. This insight would become crucial to my own subsequent startup success.

THE SCALE FALLACY REVISITED

Consultancy is the unsexy part of business. There are hundreds of best-selling books about how to make a business succeed, not so many about how to help *other* people make *theirs* succeed.

Startups have a classical narrative arc: they start small, aim high, and either succeed heroically or fail in the face of insurmountable odds. Consultancies help other businesses do business—that's not so obvious, or dramatic, a story.

I never intended to be a consultant, or to own and run a consultancy. But without the consultancy, I would likely never have had the success I've had as an entrepreneur. Consultancy provided me with an invaluable bedrock for my own projects and an unbeatable learning ground.

As well as teaching me product development and market-testing skills, consultancy taught me about managing people.

In the startup environment, your "customer" (i.e., the person you most need to satisfy) is often your investor. (This in itself is a fallacy, as we have seen—the Investment Fallacy. Investors are not valid proxies for customers. But all too often they are treated as such.) Real customers are often a long way down the line. But in consultancy, you're dealing immediately with real customers, and you have to keep them happy.

Startups tend to be driven by the shared passion of a small group of founders, who are willing to push themselves to burn out in pursuit of their project. By definition, that's not sustainable.

They're driven by passion to the exclusion of pragmatism. That can only take you so far. It may take you to the cusp of success, but it can rarely manage that success to the best effect. When people burn out, they lose perspective. They make bad decisions. Teams tear themselves apart.

Then, when a startup enters the consolidation phase, the

leadership commonly overreacts to the earlier chaos and becomes overly cautious. Original team members grow disillusioned. The company loses its spark.

I tried to combine the best of both worlds in our consultancy: the intimacy, collegiality, and creative fire of a startup with the sustainability and family-friendly environment of a more stable company. Using the company as a development lab for my own projects (and those of other team members) helped keep everyone stimulated and the atmosphere creative and supportive.

Consultancies aren't immune to the business cycle, but they can have an intrinsic countercyclical thrust. In a boom, you can scale up, but only as quickly as you can hire. In a bust, you can cut your margins and cut staff, responding immediately to the changing market rather than relying on economic forecasts. One of the virtues of consultancies is that they can do well in a downturn by helping the larger companies around them downsize, streamline, cut costs, and gain efficiency.

Services businesses are good businesses. But, till recently, if you asked a typical VC to fund your professional services agency or consultancy, you'd get a resounding "no." Services businesses don't scale, which is why a VC typically won't invest.

Services businesses don't scale because they are based on manpower: to double your revenue, you need to double the hours worked. Unless there is unused capacity, that means doubling the size of your team. And that's just to achieve 2x growth. But in the tech world, where revenue is most often based on a digital product, the marginal cost of making extra copies of that product is insignificant. Tech businesses can exponentially increase revenue without necessarily needing to greatly increase manpower. So when tech businesses talk about "scaling", they commonly mean aiming for 10x or even 100x growth.

VCs are looking for many multiples of growth to make a return on the multiple businesses they'll invest in that fail. They're not interested in slow but steady growth; they want boom, and they'll risk bust (for the individual startup) to get it. (That's just another reason why investor interest is not a good guide of the potential of your startup.)

So VCs won't be interested if your startup doesn't scale, and neither will the media and neither will the public. This is because the American dream isn't a fantasy of steady, incremental growth—it's a dream of celebrity, stardom, and riches.

If you're prepared to put the dream on hold and take a cold look at your prospects, you'll realize that there are significant advantages to creating a services business—one that doesn't scale.

You'll see money on day one, instead of working towards a future payday—which may never come.

You'll learn about the cutting edge of what customers are demanding (and developing).

And this combination of revenue to play with and a sense of what is in demand can provide the perfect ingredients with which to subsequently create a successful scalable product business.

TAKEAWAY: HOW TO AVOID THE SCALE FALLACY

- Don't be seduced by the popular emphasis on scalability and success. Look at what you can do and what the people around you need. If you have skills they can use, sell them.
- Use those skills to get inside other corporate and creative environments so you can learn from other people's mistakes before you have to learn from your own.
- When you want to build your own scalable startup, build it on the foundation of your services business. It will be stronger and more nimble, and you'll have a cushion if it collapses.

FALLACY EIGHT: THE L'ORÉAL FALLACY

THE L'ORÉAL FALLACY

(AND HOW I NEARLY FAILED TO GET OUT IN TIME)

"Because you're worth it."

THE FALLACIES WE'VE DISCOVERED *so far afflict early-stage founders: they corrupt decision making at the points of founding a business, of developing a product, of managing a team, of scaling up.*

But let's say you navigate those perils successfully and steer your company to market recognition. Are you then inured to the fallacies? No. The L'Oréal Fallacy afflicts those founders who find themselves faced with an offer for their company and the chance of an exit. This is the moment many have dreamed of. But life is no respecter of dreams: the potential exit is often smaller than the founder has hoped. The founder finds himself conflicted: wanting an exit, but believing that the offer on the table undervalues his work and the potential of his company.

The L'Oréal Fallacy is the belief that you should hold out for the exit you deserve—because you're worth it.

This fallacy corrupts decision making at a crucial point—the point when monetary success is actually a tangible prospect.

First-time founders, in particular, should take their exit when they can. Get out, go on a holiday, and then get back in the game. Instead of holding out for a better exit, move on and create one with a new product.

HOW I NEARLY FAILED TO GET OUT IN TIME

Suddenly, after years of failure, I was *hot*. The success of RightCart made me the archetypal "overnight success" that has actually been ten years in the making.

People wanted to talk to me about "the future of social shopping." Investors wanted in on the action. Other founders wanted to talk shop. But I wanted out.

As I toured boardrooms seeking an acquirer for RightCart, it seemed obvious that Amazon would be the best fit. I met with their CTO, Werner Vogels, in the fall of 2005.

I pitched him our e-commerce idea, expecting him to be enamored. Instead, he told me to stop thinking of Amazon as an e-commerce company because, under his watch, they were going to become a technology company. They would not be a buyer for RightCart.

At that time, Amazon had quietly launched something called Simple Storage Service (S3). This allowed techies to use Amazon like a giant disk drive that would never forget anything.

Not only is Amazon the largest online retailer, but it is also one of the oldest. They had been running the largest e-commerce site on the planet for, at that time, twelve years. This meant that they needed to be good at storing data. In developing its own solutions for storing vast quantities of data, Amazon (under Vogels) had realized that those solutions would be of value to the market. And, ultimately, that data storage could be of more value than its retail business.

But this was still the early days of that journey—a journey that Amazon was only starting to realize it was on. They would soon become a pioneer in cloud computing, but the term "cloud computing" had not yet even been coined.

Still, Vogels had given me a glimpse of the future. I immediately saw that Amazon's data storage services could herald a revolution.

Unlike the earlier revolution of "Web 2.0" and SaaS (software as a service), this time I was ahead of the crowd. I could see the systemic change coming.

I started using Amazon's storage services for RightCart. Even though Amazon was in the vanguard of this area, it was not yet actually a "tech" company in practice. Besides storage, web tech required servers and networking, and Amazon hadn't yet fully developed those. Their technology was rudimentary. So I built my own tools to help soften its rough spots.

Initially, these tools were purely for my own use, but, like Amazon, I soon saw that they could have market value. I merged the tools in a "dashboard" for managing Amazon's cloud services and formed a company with a colleague, Thorsten von Eicken, to commercialize it. We called it RightScale.

We hired Michael Crandell—the guru who had introduced me to the utility of landing pages (see Fallacy Four) —as CEO and gave him an equity share.

The industry as a whole was skeptical of the value of early cloud services: the experts thought the inevitable security issues would make it difficult to build consumer confidence in the cloud (the Expert Fallacy again). But to the San Francisco founder and VC communities, it was clear that the cloud would be a new horizon. If I had thought I was hot with the recognition that RightCart gained, this was on a different scale.

Almost instantly, Crandell had an offer of $4 million of investment for the business. And I was approached with offers to buy my shareholding—at up to three times its market value. Suddenly, it looked like this was going to be my long-awaited multimillion-dollar exit.

In the meantime, though, once Crandell had come on board as CEO, I had stepped back from the day-to-day to concentrate on other projects. And then I got a call to come in for a meeting.

I knew a funding round was imminent, but I hadn't heard from the team in weeks. I sensed what was coming: a cram down.

Von Eicken and Crandell sat me down and said they wanted to rebalance the equity in the company to reflect their greater workload and long-term commitment to it.

I went in to the meeting anticipating this and willing to settle for a smaller share. But they pushed harder than I expected. I gave in. I left the meeting owning just 10 percent of the company I had cofounded.

A year later, I decided to realize some of the value of that 10 percent and sell a portion of my shareholding. But they refused to release the shares.

Then they offered me a deal: they would release them, but only if I sold them to their existing investors at a value of less than one-third of what I had been offered.

I called my attorney. He laid out my options:

1. Settle and accept their offer.
2. Hold the stock, despite having no control or influence over the company's management and direction.
3. Sue them and suffer the damage to the company's value and to my reputation.

I was caught in a Catch-22. To get what I believed to be my "fair share" of the stock, I would have to sue them. But suing them would lower the value of the stock.

I was furious. I had been in their homes, and they in mine. We knew each other's families. I had brought them together—and they had ambushed me. But angry as I was at the devaluation of my stock, I was more hurt that they so devalued my contribution to creating and building the company.

Either way, they had called my bluff. I took their offer and walked with just short of a million dollars.

That was far less than I was worth on paper. It was far less again than I had been worth before I had agreed to allow my shareholding to be reduced to 10 percent.

It was also far less than typically commands respect in the sector. A million-dollar exit does not generate the attention of the tech press or accolades from the founder and VC community.

I had been lulled into anticipating a multimillion exit—one that would make my name and fortune. At first, I struggled to accept that I had been denied that by some unseemly corporate wrangling. I questioned if had I made the right decision.

But as I dedicated myself to other projects—free of the mental weight of the RightScale politicking, and now protected by a million-dollar cushion—I realized that I had made precisely the right decision. And I had learned a valuable lesson in the process: don't hold out for your ideal exit.

The mistakes had come earlier, and it took me years to recognize them and to be able to see things from the other side. The top-tier VCs that von Eicken and Crandell were courting did not want a substantial portion of the stock—and the associated financial reporting rights—in the hands of third parties. Having an absentee shareholder who was committed to other projects rather than the company could prejudice future financing rounds. And in any case, my early contribution to the company diminished in importance as time went on: I had put in the first sprint, but those who were building the company and steering it to steady success were putting in the real hard yards.

I wasn't wrong to divert to other projects: that, I learned, is my strength. And I wasn't wrong to divest substantial equity when I did so; although that laid the seed of my subsequent forced exit, it also laid the seed for the company's success. Where I went wrong, I think, was in simple personal relations. As I had done previously with the VCs backing my games studio turned dot-com (see Fallacy Three), I had failed to keep key people abreast of my movements and my plans. That meant that when I sought to divest my stock and break with the company, it came as a shock. Both sides reacted badly and relations broke down. That was unnecessary, and it hurt.

Today, RightScale has hundreds of employees and von Eicken and Crandell continue to run the company. I have no doubt they will steer it to even greater success and an incredible outcome for them personally. My journey took me elsewhere, and I have no regrets about that. My only regret is that I lost the friendship of two teammates and mentors.

THE L'ORÉAL FALLACY REVISITED

As an angel investor and a mentor and friend to younger founders, I'm regularly exposed to founders faced with an offer for their company or their stock.

This should be a cause for celebration. More often, it's a source of stress.

This is typically their first encounter with a company valuation—the first time they have a concrete value put on their share, and the prospect of converting that share into cash.

Most founders, in my experience, think that cash value is embarrassingly low. It may be $100,000, $1 million, or $10 million—irrespective of the figure, they will quote it to me with something approaching derision, as if I might think them insane for being tempted by it.

Their perspective is distorted by two things in particular: one to do with the *past* of the company and the other to do with its *future*.

How the founders' perspective on their startup's value is distorted :

BY THE PAST:
Only they know truly how much they have put into the company, how dependent it is on them, how difficult it has been to get this far. They overvalue their own input and therefore the company as a whole.

BY THE FUTURE:
Precisely because they are excessively aware of how much they have shaped the company's past, they fail to realize how dynamic and unpredictable is its future. The team, board,

and investors may have facilitated the vision of the founders to this point, but that can change: their work may inhibit or obstruct the founders' vision in the future (particularly if there is a conflict between the ambitions of investors and the founders). Unpredictable events, from economic crises to terrorist attacks to natural disasters, can knock markets radically off course. Closer to home, competitors can emerge and market trends can shift, greatly altering the perceived value of a company. Because the founders have already successfully nursed the company through a series of obstacles, they underestimate the size of the obstacles ahead.

But let's say your perspective on these things *hasn't* been distorted—but you still think the value being placed on your stake is too low—it is *objectively* too low, in other words. *Take the offer*, I say.

- It proves you have a cool business head; hubris drives too many founders to self-implode in pursuit of vainglorious ideas of their worth.
- It proves you can take a business from conception to exit.
- It frees you to go back and start again, celebrating the raw creativity of tech entrepreneurialism unhindered by the accumulated expectations of a team and investors.
- It gives you a cash cushion to support that.

You can boost your exit value through concrete, commonsense steps, such as strategically approaching potential competitors rather than blindly taking the first offer.

But be careful not to blow that first offer by treating it with derision. It may be the best offer you get. It may be the only offer you get.

Most importantly, it's a chance to prove to the market (and yourself) that you're a closer. You're not simply another founder with dreams that are deeper than the market's pockets. You're someone who has developed and delivered a startup to an exit—a rare thing.

It may not have made you a millionaire. You may not be ready to retire. But why would you want to retire? This is what you *do*.

An exit gives you the chance (and some funds) to start again. You've had your first success: the second should be easier. Better to be out there creating anew than stewing over your first creation and trying to sweat the maximum return from it.

I've stopped relying on what I think I'm worth. My equity is worth what the market will pay and only worth that when the market will pay it.

TAKEAWAY: HOW TO AVOID THE L'ORÉAL FALLACY

- It doesn't matter how much work you've put in or how great your idea is. There is no magic sum that you are "worth." There is only what the market will pay. That will change for reasons outside your control, and it may go down as well as up.
- Take the money. And don't look back.
- So take your exit.

FALLACY NINE: THE QUALITY FALLACY

THE QUALITY FALLACY

(AND HOW I LAUNCHED TOO EARLY AND WON)

Quality means doing it right when no one is looking."
–Henry Ford

Quality is the best business plan.
– John Lasseter.

IF YOU'RE A SURGEON OR AN AIRPLANE MANUFACTURER, *I'd prefer if you skipped this chapter. But if you're a founder or part of a startup team, then this is for you.*

The Quality Fallacy is the belief that quality is a goal in itself—that your product should be as good as it can be before bringing it to market.

On the contrary, quality is a distraction. Your product should be only as good as it needs to be to be brought to market. Anything more is a waste. Waste will undermine your company in the long run and lower the chance of your product finding market success.

Focus your energies and resources where they're most needed: build a minimum viable product (MVP); then concentrate on getting that to market and getting customers to it. Think of an MVP as a "Franken-product" – something cobbled together out of whatever's lying around. My next startup was a case in point.

HOW I LAUNCHED TOO EARLY AND WON

One night in October 2008, I found myself in a bedroom of the five-star Mandarin Oriental Hotel in Munich trying to print a document.

One of the companies in which I owned a share had an offer of $14 million in new investment. They needed my signature on some re-registration documents for the shares by close of business. Or else the deal risked falling through.

It was 2:00 p.m. in Santa Barbara and 11:00 p.m. in Munich.

The counterparty wouldn't accept an electronic signature. They said it had to be hard copy or fax. I told them to fax through the documents and I'd sign them and fax them back.

I phoned down to the hotel concierge, got the fax number, sent it to my colleagues, and went down to collect the incoming fax. There was nothing.

I called the office in Santa Barbara, and they tried again. Nothing. They said they had a "sent confirmation" report. I asked the concierge.

"Oh," he said, "the fax must be broken again."

There was no scanner either. The hotel's business center was long closed.

I asked for the nearest all-night office center. The concierge looked at me as if I were mad.

This was in Munich, Germany's third largest city. Munich is home to five million people and the headquarters of numerous global brands. The city is ranked eighth in the world for Fortune 500 businesses.

But it's also in Europe. In Europe, at night, people sleep.

Back up in my room, I sat at the desk at the window and looked out on a sleeping city at midnight as I tried to work out what to do.

I told the office in Santa Barbara to scan the documents and e-mail them to me. Then I opened the paint tool on my computer and set about trying to mock up a signature on screen with the mouse.

An hour later, I had something like a generic signature, bearing only the vaguest resemblance to my own. I managed to embed it on the document and e-mail it back. I hoped that by the time the office printed it off and faxed it back to the company nobody would notice.

I was right. They didn't. The company's investor was given a faxed document with an illegible, grainy black signature beside my name at the bottom. It was perfectly adequate. The deal went through. The company was $14 million better off (in cash terms, at least).

Meanwhile, in Munich, I knew one thing: I never wanted to be in that position again.

I asked one of my consultancy teammates to take an existing piece of software we had developed and adapt it to allow a signature image to be superimposed on another image (in this case, a document).

I call this approach building a Franken-product: you take whatever old junk you have lying around and use it to cobble together a new machine—in this case, a piece of software.

Two days later, he sent me a rough version. It was just one web page with three fields: From, To, and Upload a Document.

As it happened, there were already products in the market that did this, and ours was woefully inferior.

The leading products allowed you to have your signature appear "on the dotted line" in a document. Ours, embarrassingly, couldn't do that: we put the signature on an extra page, like a notary.

Theirs supported address books and templates and advanced security features. Ours didn't.

But they didn't do a simple thing we did: our signatures looked kinda like a real written signature.

Other software used a computer font for their signatures, but told you they were secure and legal. Technically, that should have been adequate. Digital signatures had been legal since 1999 when

President Clinton signed the Digital Millennium Signature Act. So that was the legal context – but the cultural context was different. Digital signatures had not yet filtered out into the culture.

E-mails do not reassure people. Signatures do. Though faxes and scans had become broadly acceptable, people still liked to see the illegible scrawl of somebody's signature in black ink at the bottom of a document, even if, when examined closely, that signature had been pixelated by electronic copying.

This web page was my rough prototype: my minimum viable product (or MVP). We started to use it internally at my consultancy, and it was well received by clients and my team. Our consultancy clients started using the product with their own teams and customers. Then some of their customers started asking how they could use it. Those clients became an expanded alpha network—we soon had a thousand such users on free trials.

I decided it was worth taking to the next stage. So we created a landing page to advertise the product and allow people to register their interest.

That landing page offered a very simple product: it would allow you to sign documents wherever you were. You would save money because you wouldn't have to print them out. You would save time because you wouldn't have to wait for contracts to be sent in the mail or faxed or e-mailed back and forth. And the counterparty would be able to see when somebody had opened and started viewing the document to be signed, thus smoothing the sales process.

We started using Google AdWords to send traffic to the landing page. We tested everything. We tested the price point; we tested new features; we tested various pricing plans. We did all of this before we fully developed the product.

Many of the features we were testing in our pricing plans did not yet exist. Then, when we identified a price point and standard set of features at which we could attract a core group of customers, we started "backfilling" those features and building up the product. We called it RightSignature.

Our customers had given us their credit card details and agreed to be charged (at whatever plan they had signed up for). But we were just getting started and didn't want to waste time building a billing system (it was DIY back then). So we took their credit card numbers and, well, we just threw them out.

We didn't save them, and we didn't charge them - but our customers didn't know that. So we were able *to prove our business* with the bare minimum of technology behind it.

We brought RightSignature to market within ten weeks of my eureka moment in Munich. Within a year, we had hard data to show we were sitting on a business that could profit and thrive.

Two years in, we had thousands of loyal, paying, small-business customers and RightSignature won a multimillion-dollar e-signature contract from Farmers Insurance, then the largest deal of its kind.

LANDING PAGES: AN ENTREPRENEUR SUPERPOWER

A landing page is simply a web page to which the user is directed from a link elsewhere. It's the page the user lands on.

In most websites, the landing page is the home page. But in this context, the landing page is the *only* page. The landing page is set up simply to gauge interest in the subject matter.

It should normally be striking and simple, clean and bright. It will present the product or service, make an offer (whether a "free trial," a fixed price, or a subscription option) and have a simple call to action (from filling in your e-mail address to registering to giving credit card details).

Like much business advice gleaned from experience, it seems incredibly simple. It *is* incredibly simple. What makes it worth giving space to is how powerful it is.

For this "superpower" model, you need to create a range of landing pages, giving different offers (or different presentations of the product), and you will likely need to invest in Google AdWords to send traffic to those different landing pages.

That will give you three key pieces of information:

- What attracts your customers.
- How much it costs (in advertising spend) to find them.
- How much they are willing to pay.

That will give you an immediate model for the viability of your business.

It's not infallible, of course. Depending on how much traffic you generate, the sample size may be small. And unless your test customers are paying (or think they are) and you are actually taking credit card details, you cannot know if interest expressed via your landing page and free-trial users will convert into paying customers. So the fact that your feedback suggests people are willing to pay at a rate that makes your business viable is not a *guarantee* of success.

What it does give you is almost infallible negative feedback: if you *fail* to attract potential users who are willing to pay, then your business is almost guaranteed to fail.

This simple process is a revolution in market testing. It dispenses with decades of accumulated (and expensive) expertise. It provides a shortcut that twentieth-century entrepreneurs would have salivated over.

I deal with a lot of low-budget, first-time founders. They are resistant to spending what may be a large portion of their budget—as much as $50,000—on this testing. They see that as money for product development.

But what is the point in developing a product for which there is no market? On the other hand, if you can *prove* there *is* a market (at the right price point), you'll have no difficulty raising extra finance should you need it.

Sometimes people object, saying this process seems disingenuous: the landing page may give a false impression that the product is already in existence. This is simply addressed.

Once visitors sign up on the site, send them an email that makes it clear that the product is in development and that the landing page is testing the market. Then reward them by keeping them informed and offering a discount when the product does launch.

Some people think this is anti-creative—that such

testing and automation sucks the lifeblood out of entre-preneurialism. My answer: I want to expend my creative energy on something that changes people's lives. To do that, it has to reach those people. And the way that a product does that, in this world, is through the market. Anything that helps that *supports* creativity—it doesn't undermine it. (I'll elaborate on this process at the end of Fallacy Ten.)

BUILDING A FRANKEN-PRODUCT

In the iconic novel, Frankenstein's monster is pieced together from the body parts of dead people and animals.

Our first version of RightSignature—our proof of concept—was what I like to call a Franken-product. It was cobbled together out of components we had previously developed for other products in the software equivalent of what the young scientist Victor Frankenstein does in his lab. It was ugly, but effective.

But not only do I use this approach to develop a proof of concept—I take it further. I don't hide the Franken-product in my lab, showing it only to trusted colleagues. I bring it to market.

My Franken-product is a *minimum viable product* (or MVP)—the least-developed version of the product that will actually work. Take anything else away from it and it won't function. Anything additional would be excess. If the market wants additional features, it will tell me.

Does it do the job? Yes. *Then we can use it to find out if the market wants that job done.*

THE QUALITY FALLACY REVISITED

When PostASAP failed (see Fallacy Four), Michael Crandell introduced me to the concept of market validation. The way we had approached PostASAP was anathema to him.

Building a business based purely on a good idea was for hobbyists: if there was no market out there, no matter how good the idea, there was no point. Get market validation as early as possible—that was his key insight.

As a creative, self-starter type, I had seen *building* things as the challenge and the attraction. Crandell taught me that it wasn't the building that was the challenging part: *it was the selling*. To sell something, you have to know the market wants it. To find out if the market wants the product, you have to ask it.

The Quality Fallacy is the belief that that the time to ask the market is when you can present it with a perfected product: only then will you be able to truly tell how it responds.

But by then, it may be too late to adapt to the market's response. The market may not want your "perfect" product at all; or it may want a version that you now can't afford to develop, or features that you can't afford to add on.

So the trick is to bring your product to market *as early as possible*. You should launch products when they are barely working—when they are "minimally viable": a *minimum viable product* (MVP).

People say,

If it ain't broken, don't fix it.

I say,

Even if it is broken, don't fix it.

Or as Reid Hoffman, founder of LinkedIn, puts it:

If your product isn't embarrassing when you launch it, you've launched it too late.

Put it out there. Let people work it out. Let them respond. Let them contribute to making it better.

The market is rarely what you think it is. Its response will challenge your assumptions. Making the necessary changes to your product when it is a minimum viable product will be far cheaper and easier than when it is "fully baked."

But what about customer retention? Don't worry about that till you have some actual customers. The focus at this point has to be on getting those customers—so the minimum amount of time and money should be invested in product development and the maximum in channeling customers to the product. That gives you the vital information you need: is your product viable?

If it is, then you can shift to a focus on quality and customer retention.

I'm not suggesting that founders should be lackadaisical, that they needn't *care* about their product. On the contrary, I expect them to care greatly.

They should care so much that they won't want to waste any time getting that product *wrong*. They should want to know as much as possible about what the market *wants* from their product so they can get it right and ensure its success.

People say you should be proud of what you do, and therefore you should do it as well as you can. I agree. But when that pride gets in the way of getting early feedback (because you want to perfect *your vision* of your product before you bring it to market), then that pride has turned to vanity.

You should be proud of your product and business in the *long term*. Making it a success may mean being willing to work with a Franken-product in the short term.

TAKEAWAY: HOW TO AVOID THE QUALITY FALLACY

- Your product doesn't need to be finished to bring it to market—it just needs to *work*. Build a *Frankenproduct*—a minimum viable product—as quickly and cheaply as you can and release that to the market.
- Use the market's feedback to refine your product so that you know you're working on something the market *wants*, not something you think the market needs.

HOW I LEARNED FROM MY FORMER FAILURES

By the time it came to RightSignature, the lessons I had been struggling to learn were starting to go in. I had gone through so many failures that I had started to recognize the fallacies that underlay them.

I would subsequently discover that there was an additional key fallacy—one that I had certainly flirted with in my career, but which I could see most starkly when I started investing in other people's startups. That was the Passion Fallacy, and that's next up, in Fallacy Ten. But first, here's a quick recap on the nine fallacies so far and how I surmounted them with RightSignature.

1. The Tech Fallacy

Not only did I barely touch the code (having delegated it to someone else), I kept away from the impulse to build technology for technology's sake.

2. The Democracy Fallacy

Instead of sharing equity and responsibility among the key team members (including myself), I stepped back and gave away most of my equity. I wanted to see the business thrive, and I knew the leadership should be allowed and incentivized to make that happen.

3. The Investment Fallacy

After its initial success, RightSignature was invited to present at a competitive investors' event, VentureNet, in Los Angeles. We won.

For days, we debated whether we could grow fast enough to justify taking on the burden of the investors' money.

Our data suggested RightSignature would be a *modest* success. The would-be investors predicted *greater* success. But we couldn't make the numbers work. We were not ready to risk our success to go all-or-nothing in pursuit of an investor's ambition. We turned the investment down.

4. The "Failure Is Not an Option" Fallacy

RightSignature was ultimately a great success, but that's only in easy-to-see hindsight. Along the way, we had our wins—good conversion rate data and investor interest—but we also had our losses—such as times when we lost key customers and partners.

We never treated RightSignature as if success were assured. Rather, we acted as if it could fail at any time. At our quarterly team meetings, we would discuss what would happen if we didn't make our sales and earnings goals—and how our failure plan would work, if needed.

Having that failure plan in the back pocket didn't make us more likely to fail, but it allowed us the confidence of knowing that, if it came to it, we could shut down the business cleanly. That reassurance made for a calmer, more professional startup environment—and that, in turn, may have been a factor in our success.

5. The Expert Fallacy

The nadir of the Expert Fallacy was when my own attorney refused to accept my e-signature on his documents. Had we asked his advice on RightSignature, we would have abandoned the business there and then. Like many an expert, he was so embedded in his field of expertise that he couldn't see that the society and culture around him was shifting. The experts said that legal documents needed to be signed in hard copy; we sensed the culture was shifting.

6. The Idea Fallacy

RightSignature launched into a field with at least two well-funded competitors. They had the same idea *and* were further ahead in building market awareness and taking market share. Conventional wisdom would have said we should have given up at that point. Instead, the existence of competitors simply reinforced my belief that there was a market for the product.

7. The Scale Fallacy

No business comes to life without incurring expenses. RightSignature was no exception. There were staff costs, rent, overheads, and market-testing costs. I carried those costs until the business reached profitability. And it was the fact that I had a boring, "unscalable" consultancy business that allowed me to do that.

The components for the "Franken-product" were scavenged from previous consultancy projects. Then, once we had our MVP, I was able to roll the product out to a test customer base: my consultancy's clients.

Yes, RightSignature was scalable. But it was built on the back of an unglamorous and unscalable services business.

8. The L'Oréal Fallacy
Rather than hoard my equity, I diluted my holding in order to give the leadership I had hired the incentive to drive the company forward.

9. The Quality Fallacy
We launched RightSignature as a Franken-product—or minimum viable product—cobbled together from components we already had lying around. It was ugly, but effective.

FALLACY TEN: THE PASSION FALLACY

THE PASSION FALLACY

(AND HOW I LEARNED TO SEE FAILURE COMING)

> *If you're choosing between businesses to start or products to launch, choose what you're most passionate about.*
> – Dave Lavinsky, business guru

AS I CHALKED UP A FEW SUCCESSES, *I started to seek out opportunities to invest. And as I developed my experience as an angel investor, I joined an investment fund as a venture partner, identifying opportunities for the fund.*

That allowed me to test and hone my insights into startup culture and to see it from the other side of the table. I saw legions of founders fall victim to the fallacies that had tripped me up. But most striking was the Passion Fallacy.

The Passion Fallacy is the belief that passion should drive your startup—that the magic ingredient is your belief in your product.

On the contrary, passion clouds judgment. I want to see evidence of cold, hard business acumen before I invest in a startup; that can exist alongside passion, sure, but more often founders seem to think that passion is an acceptable substitute.

Just like the one you're about to meet.

HOW I LEARNED TO SEE FAILURE COMING

A friend of a friend has asked me to meet with a young founder to give him "advice." I'd give ten to one odds that the founder is looking for *money*, not advice.

He gets off on the wrong foot. "We couldn't be more passionate about our product—let me show you the app."

I interrupt him. "Let's take a step back. Tell me about your market."

"Our market is anyone who has trash that they need picked up. Special trash that just can't wait until the next trash pickup. You know—trash that's unsightly and could fester and encourage vermin."

"How do you know the market wants this service?" (This is the *first* of my four standard questions.)

"What do you mean? This is an app that I want because I've seen this problem myself!"

If you've seen a problem yourself, then you have a sample size of one. I learned this the hard way with my early adventures (especially in Fallacy Four).

"OK. So how do you expect to get customers to your app?" (My *second* standard question.)

"That's easy. We're going to go viral."

I can't hold back my reply. "If going viral were that easy, why would anyone ever bother advertising?"

He looks put out. I explain. " 'Going viral' can happen in one of two ways. Either (1) you win the lottery, or (2) you make it a key focus of your business model and your team skill set, and you meticulously build a viral loop. Achieving either is a rare occurrence."

"Well, we'll attract customers with a great product."

"Yeah, but that very *first* customer—how will she find out about your product?" (This is a simplified version of the second question—I've brought it right back to basics. I'm beginning to realize that I'm not even going to get as far as my third and fourth standard questions.)

"If you advertise, you'll at least find out the cost of acquiring that first customer. Surely that's a starting point, at least?"

He looks at me with barely veiled contempt. Advertising is clearly beneath him at this high-concept stage.

"Well, I don't really have any money left for some advertising boondoggle. I've already spent so much on the product."

Their business costs are $50,000 per month. That includes salaries, rent, travel, overhead, services, and servers. They've been spending this for almost a year but they haven't reserved anything for advertising the product once it is complete—let alone *before* it's complete.

I have a suggestion. "Let's say you took $5,000 and spent it today on advertising. That would give you at least some indication of how easy it will be to attract these potential customers. Wouldn't that be valuable?"

"My business doesn't *need* an advertising model," he responds. "Even if our product doesn't get organic momentum, we'll be featured by Apple, and we'll partner with Greenpeace. With these partners, we'll get hundreds of thousands of customers."

He is now raising his voice. "And if you can't see that yourself, maybe you aren't a good fit as our investor."

"Whoa there!" I'm losing control of the conversation. I take a step back. "Do you want me to be *critical* or *supportive*? I'm a big fan of entrepreneuring and maybe right now you need support rather than critical advice."

He composes himself. "Look, I want you to be honest. Be critical. But I don't see why you're ignoring what I'm saying. We're going to make it big with one of these paths. If one doesn't work, we'll keep trying until we find another one that does. All I need is cash in the bank for the next twelve months. I thought you might be an investor who would appreciate our vision—an investor who would be interested in how we can change the world."

I get his vision. There's nothing wrong with it. But what he is also telling me—though he doesn't realize it—is that all his eggs are in the one basket.

His success is dependent on the whims of his potential partners. Such relationships can take years to develop; more often than not, they don't develop at all.

The model I am trying to explain to him is a *performance* model rather than a *partner* model. The essence of the performance model is that you can "force-feed" your market in order to test the performance of your product in the market from the earliest stages of its development.

Instead of waiting for your market to miraculously discover you, or for your partners or even the media to push you out to the market, you can proactively push your product into the market.

This costs money, but the expense can be modest. The crucial thing is that the return on that expense is closely monitored.

We've seen some of the elements of this already: you use Google AdWords to direct traffic to landing pages and use those to test interest in your product and get key metrics, such as price points. Then you launch a minimum viable product in order to test the market and use customer feedback to improve and reshape the product.

More broadly, the objective is to find a channel that you can use to direct potential users to your product. These potential users may be anything from visitors to a website to sign-ups to paying customers—whatever metric is appropriate for your business at this early stage. What's key is that you maximize the insights that you gain from those potential users: as well as landing pages, you can use surveys and customer interviews to test pricing, features, and even your market size.

The channel should be one where you can amplify the results, depending on how much you spend. So if you get positive initial results at a very low spend, you can then tentatively increase the spend and see if that positive response holds true.

It's like a volume knob: you start it low and then, if your early results are positive, you crank it up and see if the positive feedback holds.

If the results are negative, you try a different channel or strategy.

This cautious performance model is not mutually exclusive with the more ambitious partner model my young founder is committed to. He can retain his ambitions, but test in the meantime, learn from early traffic, and then gradually refine his offering, which will likely improve his pitch to his desired partners.

But he is convinced I'm making an excuse not to invest.

"You know what, Jonathan? If you don't want to invest, just say so. You said you'd be candid. But this business is not going to work one customer at a time. We need to get a big city all at once. If we don't, we can't manage the waste pickups and disposal. That's why we require big partners. This is a business that can't get 'half pregnant.'"

That opens the door for me to tell him bluntly what he needs to hear.

"I can appreciate your passion for your business, but I don't share that passion. For every ten founders I see walk through the door with similar ideas, nine of them require this same all-or-nothing approach. Unfortunately for you, I have the luxury to pass on those nine. The tenth? She's the one that intends to prove her product through a performance model—one that allows her to refine her product in response to the market and test the market's appetite before she commits all her resources. I'll invest in her. Every time."

Once started, it's hard for me to stop. "And, to be blunt, if you can't bring this product to life with baby steps, one foot in front of the other, I'd consider shelving it. There are so many ideas out there and problems to solve, why pick one that handicaps you from the start?"

At this point, the founder is ready to stand up, shake my hand, and get the hell out of my office.

THE PASSION FALLACY REVISITED

"Facebook for dogs."

"EBay for babywear."

"A mirror that tells you whether you look good."

I hear these ideas all the time.

It's not that they are intrinsically bad—or good. It's that they are barely more than that: ideas. These founders think they have a good idea. And they think their *passion* for it is what's going to convince me.

But I'm not interested in ideas. And I'm not interested in passion. In fact, passion worries me. Too often, it hides other weaknesses.

I'm interested in execution.

And "execution" doesn't mean "tech." As we've seen, the pursuit of good tech leads to the Tech Fallacy—the focus on tech for tech's sake. All I want from the tech is a clunky prototype—a Franken-product, or MVP—that allows for some market testing.

"Execution" means the ability to bring a product to market.

These founders aren't insensitive to the market. They've thought about it. Strangely enough, they commonly conclude that the market is a "billion-dollar" one. The market is always "*everybody who...*"

The market for Facebook is *everybody who* has friends. The market for Airbnb is *everybody who* travels. And so the market for these new services tends to be *everybody who* has garbage, or pets, or babies.

But the question is: how do you reach that market? How does that market learn of your existence? (There is a paradox here: a large market may *not* be a good thing. The larger the market, the harder it is to be seen by it.)

How many people in that market will be willing to pay for your service? And what will they be willing to pay?

These are *evidential* questions. The answers require

research—maybe very simple research. And almost no founder I meet ever has the answers.

In fact, they tend to get offended when I ask them. They bring me an idea backed by passion, and they expect me to invest based on the strength of those two things. They feel undermined by an approach that takes a colder, harder look.

It's easy to get blinded by the idea you're passionate about—to be fixated on your fix. It's only natural to assume that there are others out there like you seeing the same problem and wishing there was a ready-made solution to it.

And there may well be many others. But are they willing to pay for it? And can you even find them to ask them?

The Passion Fallacy is the belief that your passion should determine what you bring to market, and drive it there. It shouldn't. You are your worst test market because you are a market of one.

TAKEAWAY: HOW TO AVOID THE PASSION FALLACY

- Don't get blinded by your passion. Test a minimum viable product—no matter how ugly—on the market. And be prepared to dump it (or at least file it away) if the market isn't interested.

THE PERFORMANCE MARKETING MODEL

There are four things you need to know when building a new product:

1. ***Do people want it?***

2. ***How much will it cost to find them?***

3. ***How much are they willing to pay for it?***

4. ***How many of them are there?***

These are the four standard questions I ask every founder I meet. If you're going to ask me for advice or investment, I expect you to come with the answers. How do you get the answers? Here's a simple five-step process.

 STEP ONE: LANDING PAGE

Make a landing page—a simple, single-page website where you can advertise the product and collect potential customer information. At the very least, you'll need their e-mail—or even their phone number. Make sure the landing page creator sends these to you after every sign-up. You should create at least two variations of the same landing page for testing different pitches.

② STEP TWO: TRAFFIC

Use your creativity to get traffic to your landing pages. Maybe you have a blog that has a captive audience. Maybe you can get a partner to send an e-mail blast. Or you can always pay Google, Facebook, LinkedIn, and Twitter to send you relevant traffic.

③ STEP THREE: FIRST ANALYSIS

You should be at this step within a month. You can now answer the first question: Do people want your product? If so, then it's time to think about pricing. Your optimal pricing will depend on your costs, what your competitors are charging, and what your potential customers will pay. Ask them: add a survey to the landing page, or contact them individually.

④ STEP FOUR: PRICING

Now you add pricing to your landing pages. This can be as simple as adding another line to the page right above the sign-up. For example, "Sign up now and get your early access discount of $99 per month."

It's just a test, so be bold. I typically put a ridiculously low price and a ridiculously high price in the mix on separate landing pages. This will give you data points on your pricing curve. A pricing curve can be seen if you take a piece of graph paper and plot the price you are charging in a test versus the sign-up rate for the test.

Having two or three data points on this curve will put you head and shoulders above everyone else in your entrepreneurial peer group.

5 STEP FIVE: FINAL ANALYSIS

You now have all the data you need to answer my first three questions. The answer to question four—how many potential customers are there—will come from Google if you have used their AdWords service. You'll have paid them for a set amount of click-throughs on a key ad word. Their dashboard will give you a figure for the total number of searches for that ad word—that gives a very rough indication of the size of the potential market.

There are a *lot* of assumptions underlying this: that sign-ups will convert to customers (many won't), that customers will remain with you for a particular duration (they may not), and that potential customers won't be deterred by being used as market guinea pigs (if you design your tests well, they won't). This is social science, not hard science.

Still, this data will help you hugely in making a success of your business—or, critically, in anticipating its failure. It may not be foolproof, but it's a damn sight better than no data. It is inexcusable not to pursue it.

The Buddhist monk Thich Nhat Hanh writes:

> If I lose my direction, I have to look for the North Star, and I go to the north. That does not mean I expect to arrive at the North Star. I just want to go in that direction.

Market testing is no guarantee of success. But it certainly helps you go in that direction.

THE FALLACIES
OF SAN FRANCISCO

WHAT KNOWLEDGE OR INSIGHTS I have come from a past filled with following dead ends. When I meet new founders, I want to share the lessons of my mistakes and failures so they can avoid them.

Yet I still find myself struggling to follow my own advice. Some of these fallacies are simply in my nature; some of them are in the ether – in San Francisco and throughout our sector. They are cultural forces, and they can exert a hold even when you guard against them.

So let's recap on the ten fallacies I have stumbled upon (often painfully) in my career.

THE TEN FALLACIES THAT MADE THIS FOUNDER FAIL

Fallacy One: The Tech Fallacy

The belief that your technology is all-important.

Founders too often fall down a tech cul-de-sac—or rabbit hole—where they focus on their tech problem to the exclusion of all else. Worry about the market first – finessing the tech can come later (if at all).

Developing technology is expensive. Finding out if there's a market for that tech can be much cheaper.

Fallacy Two: The Democracy Fallacy

The belief that good teams—and therefore startup companies—should share leadership and equity.

Shared leadership slows down decision making. Shared equity blunts incentives. Democracy works for countries, for communities, and even for some long-established cooperative businesses. It doesn't work for startups.

Fallacy Three: The Investment Fallacy

The belief that securing investment is a mark of achievement.

You just have to read the tech press to see how pervasive this is: stories trumpeting some firm's success in raising Series A or B funding are a staple.

Rarely stressed is the potential downside: greater pressure on the business, a diluted stake for the founders and often legal obstacles to cashing that stake in, and, most ominously, misaligned investor and founder incentives.

Avoid taking investment as far as possible. If it becomes unavoidable, monitor yourself to make sure you manage it right. You need to look after your investors without letting them subvert the focus of the company.

Fallacy Four: The "Failure Is Not an Option" Fallacy

The idea that success comes to those who refuse to consider failure.

This runs right through American public life. Perhaps it has a place in sport (though I doubt it is *ever* healthy). But in business, it is positively damaging. We all prefer to succeed than fail, but failure is an almost inevitable step on the path to success.

How you fail may determine your likelihood of succeeding in the future. Failure always hurts, but it makes sense to minimize the damage. That means planning ahead. Make a Failure Plan.

When I invest in a startup, I ask the founder what his or her plan for failure is. Most just say they're planning for success. The ones who can explain how they'll manage failure, as well as how they intend to avoid it, are the ones that convince me.

Fallacy Five: The Expert Fallacy

The belief that the experts know best.

Obviously, there is a place for this: in rocket science, in medicine, in Nascar racing.

But be wary of the experts in startups and in technology in particular. By definition, a disruptive technology can have no pre-existing experts.

Experts become experts because of their dedication to a field of study, which is a good thing in itself. But it's precisely that dedication that makes them singularly unqualified to anticipate challenges to the basis of that field of study: systemic change.

Fallacy Six: The Idea Fallacy

The idea that inspiration counts more than perspiration.

It may be surprising that this fallacy is so pervasive, given that its damaging consequences are so ingrained in Silicon Valley's self-aware-ness. The Idea Fallacy was at the root of the dot-com bust of 2001: too much capital behind too many ideas with not enough market.

But the Idea Fallacy is deeply ingrained in the broader culture and in all of the creative industries. It's the idea that genius is some-thing that happens in eureka moments rather than over tens of thousands of hours of relentless practice and experimentation.

Fallacy Seven: The Scale Fallacy

The belief that the only thing that counts in the tech startup world is a product that can scale.

This is probably symptomatic of the influence of venture capital, which has long demonstrated a preference for companies that can scale over companies where growth is, at best, steady - product companies rather than services companies.

I discovered services as a teenager. Consulting helped me pay my way through college, experiment with early startups, skill up through working with clients on cutting-edge products, and consistently gave me a bedrock of support and a safety net of income as I failed and failed again with my own product startups.

Fallacy Eight: The L'Oréal Fallacy

The belief that you shouldn't accept anything less than you're "worth".

This fallacy is more selective: it afflicts those who have already had a degree of success. But, precisely for that reason, it can be more damaging.

Our sector uses money as a metric of success: the size of an exit or of a valuation or of a funding round. That leads people to aim for figures that have no concrete relation to their business.

Your business is worth what someone will pay for it. Your equity is worth what someone will pay for it, *if* you can release it. Pay no attention to what you're worth "on paper," and don't be driven by the expectations of others (or your younger self) as to what success is. If you get a timely offer that will help you take on other challenges, take it.

Fallacy Nine: The Quality Fallacy

The idea that quality is a higher moral goal; that you should focus on quality first.

This is another fallacy with deep cultural roots. In the wider culture, of course, there is much to be said for the pursuit of quality for its own sake.

But in the tech startup sector, such focus on absolute quality can be distracting, at best, and destructive, at worst. Startups should set their expectations on a minimum viable product—an MVP. Only if and when that gets traction in the market sufficient to fund its development is there room to focus on quality.

Fallacy Ten: The Passion Fallacy

The belief that passion is the key ingredient behind an idea and a product.

This, like the Tech Fallacy, is endemic. The point is not that you should *not* be passionate about your product; rather, you do not *need* to be passionate about it, and your passion is not necessarily a selling point.

As an investor, I want to see that you, the founder, have the capacity to *execute*. Passion often obscures a failure to plan rigorously. Most insidiously, it can blind founders to the weaknesses in their own products and strategies.

THE SAN FRANCISCO FALLACY REVISITED

On the face of it, the San Francisco Fallacy may seem trivial by comparison with the ten fallacies we've just examined. A piece of geographical advice—*"Don't move to San Francisco"*—hardly ranks up there with core lessons of business.

But the San Francisco Fallacy is symptomatic of a broader and deeper danger in the culture—the danger of groupthink. The urge to base tech startups in San Francisco is a very literal example of herding behavior, whereby members of a community have an instinctive tendency to follow each other.

All of the other fallacies stem in some way from this, because all of them draw their force from the fact that they are beliefs widely shared in the society around them. Consensus and conformism exert a powerful pull on people, even on those who self-identify as outsiders or mavericks.

We're all subject to this—as I've shown, I am no exception. Seeing through groupthink and spotting these fallacies for what they are isn't simply a question of a momentary insight. It requires constant, rigorous analysis of your market, of your product, of your company, of your team, and of yourself.

The ultimate reward for this approach to your startup is success—perhaps not storybook success, but success you can measure, success you can share, success you can build upon, and success you can build a life around.

There is no magic trick. This has not been a book of hard and fast rules. Fallacies are cultural beliefs; they don't come with tricks of the trade to avoid them.

Watching out for them requires observation, discipline, rigor, smarts, and emotional intuition. Reacting to them requires judgment and balance.

The lessons in them won't all be correct for you, all of the time. Overcorrecting for one could leave you exposed to another: as we've seen, the dominance of the Idea Fallacy led the market to overcorrect and resulted in the dominance, for a time, of the Tech Fallacy.

This kind of analysis will always be more difficult if you surround yourself with people whose interests, culture, and working environments are the same.

Seeing through groupthink requires you to stand apart from the herd. In the first place, that's a mental and emotional discipline. But it doesn't help if you live and work *surrounded* by the herd.

San Francisco is an overpriced, underperforming bubble.

Leave the storybook stuff to the dreamers thinking up great ideas over overpriced coffees in the city's cafes.

Find somewhere cheaper, with better talent, that is more in touch with the mainstream. Build your business based on the values in this book, not on desire, dreams, or passion.

But of course, you'll need something else—something no book can give you and no experience can guarantee:

Good luck.

ABOUT THE AUTHOR

JONATHAN SIEGEL is the founder of RightCart, RightSignature, and RightScale. He is chairman and founder of Xenon Ventures, which specializes in the acquisition, acceleration, and exit of high-margin Software as a Service companies. He spent ten years as the founder and CEO of ELC Technologies, a Ruby on Rails consultancy, which was acquired in 2010 by PriceGrabber's Kamran Pourzanjani. He also has a sideline as the founder of a chain of Irish pubs on the West Coast, Brendan's. Following the mantra, "If something is important, do it yourself," he is a patent author, a licensed real estate broker, a licensed contractor, a FAA-certified flight instructor (MEI, CFII fixed wing land), a certified helicopter private pilot, and a certified commercial jet pilot (EA50). He has lived in Santa Barbara, Las Vegas, San Francisco, Dublin, and Tokyo with his wife and a growing number of Irish-American children (currently eight).

ABOUT THE ILLUSTRATOR

FIACHRA LENNON is an Irish illustrator, designer, and developer who likes doing fun stuff with the family, drawing, making websites, designing things, playing music, playing and watching sports, traveling, and learning. He would like to do more things, but sure, there's only so many hours in one day.

@FiachraLennon

www.fiachralennon.com

49051926R00082

Made in the USA
San Bernardino, CA
11 May 2017